what do we know and what should we do about...? BMA

the future of work

Melanie Simm

Los Angeles | London | New Delhi
Singapore | Washington DC | Melbourne

SAGE Publications Ltd
1 Oliver's Yard
55 City Road
London EC1Y 1SP

SAGE Publications Inc.
2455 Teller Road
Thousand Oaks, California 91320

SAGE Publications India Pvt Ltd
B 1/I 1 Mohan Cooperative Industrial Area
Mathura Road
New Delhi 110 044

SAGE Publications Asia-Pacific Pte Ltd
3 Church Street
#10-04 Samsung Hub
Singapore 049483

Editor: Matthew Waters
Editorial assistant: Jasleen Kaur
Production editor: Katherine Haw
Copyeditor: Neville Hankins
Proofreader: Clare Weaver
Indexer: Charmian Parkin
Marketing manager: George Kimble
Cover design: Lisa Harper-Wells
Typeset by: C&M Digitals (P), Chennai, India
Printed in the UK

Library of Congress Control Number: 2019938000

British Library Cataloguing in Publication data

A catalogue record for this book is available from the British Library

ISBN 978-1-5264-6345-6
ISBN 978-1-5264-6346-3 (pbk)

At SAGE we take sustainability seriously. Most of our products are printed in the UK using responsibly sourced papers and boards. When we print overseas we ensure sustainable papers are used as measured by the PREPS grading system. We undertake an annual audit to monitor our sustainability

contents

titles in the series

about the series

Every news bulletin carries stories which relate in some way to the social sciences – most obviously politics, economics and sociology but also, often, anthropology, business studies, security studies, criminology, geography and many others.

Yet despite the existence of large numbers of academics who research these subjects, relatively little of their work is known to the general public. There are many reasons for that but one, arguably, is that the kinds of formats that social scientists publish in, and the way in which they write, are simply not accessible to the general public.

The guiding theme of this series is to provide a format and a way of writing which addresses this problem. Each book in the series is concerned with a topic of widespread public interest, and each is written in a way which is readily understandable to the general reader with no particular background knowledge.

The authors are academics with an established reputation and a track record of research in the relevant subject. They provide an overview of the research knowledge about the subject, whether this be long-established or reporting the most recent findings; widely accepted or still controversial. Often in public debate there is a demand for greater clarity about the facts, and that is one of the things the books in this series provide.

However, in social sciences, facts are often disputed and subject to different interpretations. They do not always, or even often, 'speak for themselves'. The authors therefore strive to show the different interpretations or the key controversies about their topics, but without getting bogged down in arcane academic arguments.

Not only can there be disputes about facts but also there are almost invariably different views on what should follow from these facts. And, in any case, public debate requires more of academics than just to report facts; it is also necessary to make suggestions and recommendations about the implications of these facts.

Thus each volume also contains ideas about 'what we should do' within each topic area. These are based upon the authors' knowledge of the field but also, inevitably, upon their own views, values and preferences. Readers may not agree with them, but the intention is to provoke thought and well-informed debate.

Chris Grey, Series Editor

Professor of Organization Studies

Royal Holloway, University of London

about the author

Melanie Simms is Professor of Work and Employment at the University of Glasgow, UK. She writes widely on the topic of work and employment with a particular interest in two main areas: how workers get to influence changes at work; and how young people move into the labour market after education.

introduction

What is work?

Work is a far wider concept than simply paid employment. The focus of this book is mainly on paid employment, but there is a fuzzy line between concepts. Even paid employment is not as easy to define as we might at first think. It involves an exchange of labour for some kind of payment, but both parts of that definition are complex. Technically, what is offered by the worker is the *capacity* to work, rather than the work itself. Workers will make themselves available to the employer for a particular period of time. The job of the employer – usually through managers and control systems – is to ensure that the labour is directed at the activities required, and to an appropriate quality. Workers are people and, as such, have their own capacity to act. They may not do what the employer requires, or they may not do it to the quality needed. This process of overseeing and controlling what workers do as they work is the complex process of management.

The exchange for payment is also less simple than it may at first seem. Workers may exchange their capacity to work for a range of benefits including money, time off, holiday allowances, a pension (wages that will be returned in the future), discounted food in canteens, and a whole host of other possible perks. Most of these are additional benefits to the basic wage, but there is scope for less obviously beneficial exchanges. Many countries now have rules that require most of the payment to be in the form of currency, but there are certainly plenty of examples around the world and from history where workers have been paid in tokens that, for example, can only be exchanged for goods in the company shop.

Both the capacity to work and the payment it is exchanged for are complex ideas. Things get even more blurred when we think about the boundaries between work and non-work activities. Should we include things like work travel as part of our work time that should be compensated? Even if we can sit back on an aeroplane, drink a gin and tonic and watch Netflix? What about time spent commuting to work? And what if we have to buy a uniform or special clothes to wear to work? Every job has fuzzy boundaries, which always introduces the idea that what we choose to define as 'work' or even as 'paid employment' is contested and always subject to negotiation and renegotiation both at the level of individuals and as a society.

Paid employment is at the centre of our interest here. Of course, there are many forms of work that are unpaid, and these are important to acknowledge. Slavery is an important example. Modern slavery exists in areas such as domestic labour where workers can be brought to the UK to do the childcare and household tasks for a large family, but the terms of the exchange are not freely chosen. Undoubtedly this is work – hard work. The lack of freedom to choose to enter or leave the employment relationship, plus the lack of clear payment for the work done, mean that it falls into a category beyond our consideration here. Private unpaid domestic labour within a family or household is also really important in keeping the lives of workers going. Someone has to wash the clothes and cook the dinner before workers can leave the house and move into the workplace. Even now, this work is mainly done by women, even in households where the women also undertake paid employment. A recent report by the Office for National Statistics (2016) showed that women do, on average, around 26 hours of unpaid domestic labour a week, compared with 16 hours done by men. It is crucially important work, but it is not usually done for a wage as part of an employment relationship, so it is not the focus here. Again, there are fuzzy boundaries.

What is viewed as legitimate labour can also change over time. There has recently been growing public concern about unpaid interns. These recruits are not paid, but they usually work in a workplace alongside paid staff and do similar tasks. In exchange for giving their labour, they gain experience about the industry and/or about work in general. For a young person trying to break into a particular sector, this experience can be really important. But increasingly as a society, we have come to understand that this approach to work experience risks deepening social divides because often the only people who can afford to give up their time for free in this way already have a lot of resources, usually within their family. Those family resources help provide accommodation, food, travel, work clothes and all the other costs that are required to be able to go to work. So, in areas such as the creative industries, fashion, magazine writing and similar where unpaid internships are common, there have been growing voices warning that this risks perpetuating systems that mean only people with the privilege of family support can gain the kinds of work experience necessary to make it in these industries. While this raises important social questions to understand how unpaid internships help explain why particular professions and sectors struggle to recruit a more diverse workforce, it is not the main focus of this book because it takes us beyond the boundaries of paid employment.

This brings into focus another key concept: the employment relationship. This can be understood as the relationship between a paid worker or employee and the person or organisation that employs them. In exchange for the payment, the employer's role is to try to make sure that the worker uses their skills and capacity for whatever objectives and quality are required. Central to understanding the employment relationship is the fact that it is constantly in a state of flux; the 'give and take' is always under negotiation from both sides. This idea that work is about social as well as economic relationships and exchanges is really important because it helps to remind us that it is always about people and not simply about the legal contract someone signs when they start work, or the economics of the decision to apply for a particular job. People have different understandings of the situations they find themselves in and they have different interests. As we shall see, generally speaking, individual workers usually have less power in the employment relationship than their employers. These features make the employment relationship between workers and their employers messy and requiring ongoing negotiation. So, negotiation – sometimes explicit, sometimes implicit – about what a worker is able and/or willing to do in exchange for the payment they receive is at the heart of the employment relationship.

Who works?

The focus of this book is paid employment in the UK. The Labour Force Survey tells us that just over 32.5 million people work in the UK from a total population of around 65.6 million. (Unless otherwise mentioned, all of the statistics in this section come from the UK Labour Force Survey which is explained in more detail in the further reading section at the end of the book). Of course, like all statistics about complex social issues, this hides a number of judgements about what is measured and how. The first point about measuring employment statistics is the idea of a *working age population*. In the UK, we tend to measure the proportion of people who work in the age group between 16 (when compulsory education ends) and 64. Around 75% of that population work. That figure is quite high when you consider the number of people who stay in education beyond the age of 16; the fact that a lot of people take time out of the labour market to provide care for children and other relatives; the number of people who are unable to work because of illness and other situations; and that many people reduce their engage-ment with the labour market before the age of 64. All of these can create complex patterns of employment and unemployment across someone's life course.

Politicians are usually most worried about the *unemployment level*, which in 2018 in the UK was around 1.38 million. Unemployment is defined as being available for work, but not being in work. Most observers are not particularly worried about small levels of unemployment because it is normal for some people to have short periods of unemployment as they decide to move between jobs, or as they look for a different job if they lose their job. What is particularly concerning to policy makers are people who have extended periods of unemployment, which is usually taken as meaning six months or more. This is because people who are unemployed for a relatively long time can struggle to re-enter the labour market for a number of reasons, including the fact that their skills become out of date, and they lose confidence and experience. Around 573,000 people in the UK fall within this definition. This puts the *unemployment rate* for people aged 16 and over around 4.1%.

Academic commentators also point out that the definition of unem-ployment is not always helpful in understanding in detail what is happening in the labour market. Many people find themselves without work but are not formally defined as unemployed. A good example here that has gained a lot of attention in recent debates is someone who is employed on a zero-hours contract (ZHC) but who is not allocated any work for a period of time. Zero-hours contracts are formally a contract of employment, but do not guarantee any particular hours being allocated in a particular week or month. So a worker may go for some time without being allocated any paid work. These workers are therefore formally employed but not given work. Another example is self-employed workers, which we will return to later.

Unemployment is also a very different measure from the number of people claiming various social security payments for unemployment. The latter is measured by a figure called the *claimant count*. Any government can put in place rules that people must adhere to in order to claim social security, and this inevitably means that there will be a gap between the number of people who are unemployed and the number who can claim unemployment payments. In recent years, the rules about claiming unemployment payments in the UK have become gradually stricter, so there is now a large gap between the number of people claiming out-of-work benefits (around 924,600) and the much higher figure of around 1.38 million who are counted as being unemployed.

A further group of people we need to think about are those people who are *economically inactive*. In other words, they could potentially work but are currently either not seeking work or not available to start work in the next two weeks. There are currently 8.66 million economically inactive people in the age range 16–64 in the UK. They include students, people whose main responsibility is household work or unpaid care, and people who have some other income not from employment (perhaps from having sold a company, from investments, or similar).

These measures about who 'counts' as employed, unemployed or economically inactive are really important in public debates about work and employment. Most governments are particularly concerned about measures of unemployment as the headline indicator of the state of the labour market. But we can see even from the brief discussion above that there are big societal changes that can easily influence those headline figures. One example is that it is now far more common than it was 50 years ago for young people to extend their time in education beyond the age of 16. This has changed the labour market in lots of complex ways. Even when students are working, most of them are classified as students – and therefore economically inactive – for the purposes of official statistics. This has the effect of changing the data about the flows of young people into the labour market.

Similarly, it is now far more common for women to re-enter the labour market after they have had children. Even 50 years ago, this was quite difficult in many occupations, yet today is seen as perfectly normal, although we need to remember that those women often face challenges in progressing in their careers, especially if they work part-time. Again, this changes who is available for work, and how they want to work. Perhaps unsurprisingly, alongside this huge change in social norms a demand has arisen for work that better suits people who are caring for young families, namely part-time work, flexible work and similar. So, while employers now have a far larger pool of people in their 30s and 40s to recruit from, there have been gradual pressures to change some of the kinds of work offered.

This highlights a central point of this book: when we talk about work, employment and the labour market, we must never assume that it is fixed or static in any way. Employers, (potential) workers and governments make choices and respond to each other's choices. The example above is a good one. As more women have entered the labour market, employers and governments have responded. Sometimes they have freely chosen to respond, at other times they have been forced to respond by changes to the law on equal pay or other laws giving women access to equal treatment at work. The three main actors in employment – the government, employers and workers – therefore interact in a constantly moving situation. As a result, the exchange between workers and employers is negotiated and renegotiated as the situation changes. Sometimes the negotiation is explicit (e.g. at the start of a job when a worker agrees to a set of terms and conditions of employment) and sometimes it is not actively noticed (e.g. an employer might decide to provide a training programme to help and encourage managers to make jobs more flexible). It is the negotiation and renegotiation of the future of employment relationships that is at the heart of this book.

We noted previously that there is another big group of workers we need to consider. In addition to the approximately 27 million people in the UK who are employees, there are a further 4.7 million who are classified as self-employed. This is a category that is surprisingly difficult to define. It includes some of the people we might typically think about when we think about self-employment: perhaps a plumber who runs a small business; or an IT specialist who works on a range of different projects for different companies. But there has also been a growth in the number of self-employed workers who are more difficult to categorise as definitively self-employed. They may work for only one company and may even wear the company uniform, but for tax purposes they are considered to be self-employed. For example, a lot of delivery drivers fall into this group. They may own the vehicle that they use for deliveries, but it may often be branded with the company logo and the driver may well wear a uniform of that company. If they work for the company full-time and the company tells them whether or not they can have breaks, annual leave and similar, it is difficult to argue that the person is genuinely self-employed, although they may well fall into that category for statistical purposes. Because this is a small but growing group, we will pay attention to them in this book.

There is a clear benefit to a company in using *bogus self-employed workers* because it does not have to pay for costs such as the employers' contributions to tax and National Insurance. These workers also do not have the same rights as standard employees. They have to arrange their own holiday and sick pay and are not usually covered by laws about maximum working time or minimum wages. There have been a number of high-profile legal cases recently where workers have argued – often successfully – that they should be covered by various employment rights that regular employees benefit from, such as paid sick leave. This kind of complexity arises because there are different measures used for employment data for the application of employment law and for tax purposes.

In general, then, we can see that there are always incentives to try to blur the boundaries between different groups of workers. In these cases, employers have tried to push the boundaries of what can be defined as self-employment, often in an effort to keep down costs and ensure that labour is as inexpensive and flexible as possible. This has generated a 'pushback' from individual workers and representative organisations such as trade unions who have presented legal cases to try to define these categories more clearly. This shows the negotiation and renegotiation of work and employment in action.

What do we do at work?

Official statistics measure in a number of ways the industries and sectors in which people work. One way is to look at the public and private sectors. The private sector is run by individuals and companies, usually for profit. Around 27 million workers are employed in the private sector. The public sector is work that is supported by the government via taxation. Jobs in areas such as health and social work, education, public administration and the police all fall into this group. In December 2017, around 5.3 million people were employed in the public sector. Because of reductions in government spending after the Global Financial Crisis of 2007–8, there have been many job losses in the public sector over the past decade, so this figure is considerably lower than it has been in the recent past.

Another way to look at the data about the jobs we do is to use the Standard Industrial Classification. This pays less attention to whether work is in the public or private sector, but tells us about the kinds of industries people work in. The largest industries are shown in Figure 1.1.

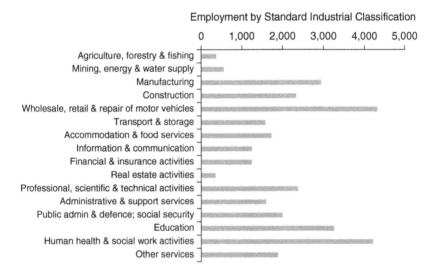

Figure 1.1

Source: Labour Force Survey, October–December 2017 ('000s employees)

The vast majority of workers (around 23.9 million from the total of 32.4 million) are working full-time and about 8.5 million part-time.

On average across all workers, people worked 32 hours per week in 2017. Of those who are classified as full-time, the average was 37 hours, while part-timers worked an average of around 16 hours per week. This fits what might be regarded as a 'normal' expectation of full-time and part-time work, but it hides some surprising figures. Returning to the previous point about self-employment being a varied category, we know that more than a quarter (30%) of self-employed workers are part-time. Zero-hours and low-hours contracts are also a form of part-time work where the employer does not guarantee any work beyond the minimum. Workers on these contracts often end up working a lot longer than their contracted hours in very flexible work patterns. This can sometimes be a benefit for the workers if they have the right to reject work when it is offered, but too often employers require them to accept the work, which means the flexibility of those contracts runs only one way.

While politicians are usually most worried about the headline unemployment rate, a different way to measure potential capacity in the labour market is to look at under-employment. The Labour Force Survey estimates that over 900,000 part-time workers say that they want and could take on a full-time job, but cannot not find one. This hints at a small, but important, minority of workers who can be considered as *under-employed*. In other words, they are in employment, but they are not working as much as they would like and are able. There has always been some level of under-employment in the labour force because part-time jobs can be used as a way for employers to screen people before hiring them for full-time roles. However, there is good evidence that this pool of under-employed workers has grown in the past two decades, and this phenomenon is part of what has become known as the 'gig economy'.

How much do we earn at work?

Also important to consider is how much people earn when they are at work. The average regular pay for employees in February 2018 – excluding any bonuses – was £483 per week before tax and other deductions. The average total pay including bonuses but before tax and deductions was £513. (Data about wages published by the Office for National Statistics comes from two sources: the Annual Survey of Hours and Earnings and Average Weekly Earnings data. Again, more information about sources is available in the further reading section.) So, the average annual salary excluding bonuses was £25,116 per year, and £26,676 including bonuses. Of course, salaries are not evenly spread across the population and wage data is always skewed by the fact that a very small number of high earners can push up the averages. This concern about the pay and bonuses earned by the *top 1%* has become a topic of considerable public debate, especially as such pay has increased much more quickly than for the majority of workers in recent years.

Why does work matter?

Work matters because it is integral to the ways in which we as human beings have structured our societies. In a highly influential book called *The Thought of Work*, Professor John Budd (2011) outlines some of the functions that work fulfils for individuals and society: as a curse, as a freedom, as a commodity, as providing occupational citizenship, as a disutility, as personal fulfilment, as a social relationship, as caring for others, as identity, and as service. Even this is probably not an exhaustive list, but it highlights the different social and economic functions that work can fulfil in our lives. These multiple functions of work and employment in our societies and lives are crucially important because they bring inevitable tensions and contradictions. It is not uncommon for people to report that they like particular parts of their jobs, while also feeling burdened or constrained by the fact that they cannot act entirely freely because their time is directed by their employer and manager. A job that I might find very boring or stressful may suit another person very well indeed. These tensions and contradictions emerge from the fact that paid employment performs these multiple functions in our societies, economies and personal lives.

If we focus on paid employment, most of us live in societies where work also creates and reinforces patterns of inequalities. There is no level playing field for access to the best jobs. Nor are there equal opportunities to use income to build up wealth by, for example, paying a mortgage to buy a house, or building up pensions assets. To make a broad generalisation, the more access to these forms of wealth your parents had or have, the more likely it is that you will be able to access them yourself. So, patterns of inequality can persist not only across an individual's lifetime, but also across generations. Even in the context of public debate about the increasing inequality between younger and older generations in the UK, there remains greater inequality between the richest and the poorest in any given generation. Although some of this inequality arises from differences in wealth that is passed between generations, at least some of it results from the differences in access to different kinds of paid work: specifically, who has access to high-paid and low-paid jobs?

One particularly important period in people's lives is their transition from education to work. Opportunities for young people to find their first paid employment after education vary depending on the performance of the economy at particular moments in time. Young people who are unlucky enough to move into the labour market when there is a contraction or a recession in the economy can find their chances of finding work scarred for ever (Bell and Blanchflower, 2011). The reasons for this are complex and it is likely that there are three main effects happening. First, when the economy later picks up, these workers do not have the experience that employers would expect of someone several years after school or college. Second, a fresh batch of young people will have entered the labour market after them who are *blank slates* for employers to recruit. And third, the young people themselves may have been disheartened by their early experiences of no work or poor-quality work and may be less engaged with job seeking. What is well established is the effect of early experiences of (un)employment. As they get older, workers who experience early periods of unemployment will earn less than other cohorts, they will experience less good health, and they are more likely to die younger. All of these are proxy measures for being less wealthy and earning less across a lifetime. So, what is increasingly clear from research evidence is that early experiences of work continue to have ripple effects through someone's life – and some of that is purely down to chance.

In that context, policy makers have become very keen to try to measure *social mobility*. Social mobility can be defined as the likelihood of someone moving from one class position to a different class position over their lifetime. The idea of *class position* can sometimes be controversial, but in this kind of research it really just means someone's income and wealth which are typically measured by their occupation. In public debate, the idea of social mobility is usually regarded very positively. Many see it as shorthand for the ability of people with various kinds of disadvantage to improve their lives through access to good-quality education and jobs. But we often forget that social mobility can also mean people moving down the occupational ladder, so the children of parents who have higher income and advantage may move into occupations that are less well paid. In short, whether we see social mobility as a good thing or not, it is clearly linked to the jobs that we do.

Thus, work matters. Someone's occupational status is often the biggest influence on the amount of wealth and income they can accrue over their lifetime. This has an enormous influence on a whole range of life outcomes, including how healthy they are likely to be, how long they are likely to live, where they can live, and a range of other important life chances. The UK has relatively low levels of social mobility, so one of the most important influences on the occupation someone has is the occupational class of their parents. That is not to say that there is no social mobility – plenty of individuals move up and down the occupational groups during their working lives. But it does mean that we need to pay attention to all kinds of work and employment when we discuss the future of work because some groups have more advantages and resources than others to navigate changes. It also pushes us to pay attention to the choices that are made by employers and the state about work and how those decisions affect work and working people.

what do we know about work?

How has work changed?

Patterns of work are constantly changing and there are always reasons for politicians and commentators to highlight particular areas of change or continuity. Over the past 100 years, say, we have seen big changes in who works and what kinds of jobs they do. Ideas about equality of access to jobs and progression within a career that were unthinkable even a few decades ago are generally now widely accepted. One of the things we always need to ask ourselves when we think about how work is changing is: what time period is being discussed? Although it may seem obvious to highlight that work has changed a lot over time, the historical perspective is often invoked but rarely examined closely in public debate. It is perhaps surprising that in some respects we could argue that work has remained remarkably *stable* since the period of mass urbanisation and industrial work associated with the Industrial Revolutions of the 1880s and onwards.

This might seem a provocative view, and certainly it is not the same as arguing that *nothing* has changed. But the core structures of organising work and employment that were laid down during the Industrial Revolutions are still very evident in our day-to-day lives even in the twenty-first century. So, for example, most people go to a workplace that is outside their home and work a broadly standardised day shift of around seven or eight hours per day.

Even when we look at the industries people work in, we should remember that manufacturing is still a very important part of the UK economy, as is discussed more later. It is important to keep this continuity in mind when we talk about the future of work, as we will do in the later parts of this book. Much of people's judgement about how work might change rests on whether they think there are going to be slow changes or big social, economic and cultural shifts that will quickly and radically alter the kind of work we do and how we do it. My own view is closer to the former view: patterns of work have been relatively stable over such a long historical sweep that it would require a fundamental change in social structures before we see really big changes to the way that the majority of people work. Of course, saying that there has been remarkable stability is not to deny that there have been important changes. Looking at some key changes in the UK labour market helps outline the context of the future of work.

Women's employment

Women have always worked beyond the domestic sphere. However, women's employment patterns have particularly changed since the 1960s when a series of laws were introduced to try to facilitate more equal access to and progression at work. Three major areas of employment law in the 1970s helped ensure fairer access for women to the labour market: the Equal Pay Act in 1970, the Sex Discrimination Act in 1975, and the strengthening of maternity rights and pay. Combined, these have created a context which has reinforced the rights of women to equal treatment in the workplace and to accommodate periods of leave for maternal caregiving. Since then, women's participation in the labour market has risen steadily. In 1975 approximately 57% of women aged between 25 and 54 (what is sometimes known as *prime working age*) were employed; by 2017 that figure was 78% (Roantree and Vira, 2018).

Their study highlighted the reasons behind this notable and consistent rise of women in employment. One of the major changes has been the rise of women working in full-time employment from 29% in 1985 (when data on work hours started to be collected) to 44% in 2017. It also reflects the fact that women now have fewer children, and if they do have children it is often later in life. This means there are now more younger women in the labour market and available to work. In addition, women are far less likely to leave work if they do have a child, reflecting the practical importance of paid maternity leave to women's patterns of work. In sum, all of this means that women are now more likely than in the past to continue to work while also being parents, thus increasing the number of women in the labour force.

The kinds of roles women take on are also important in explaining patterns within the labour market. The Labour Force Survey shows us that women are far more likely than men to be employed in caring occupations such as nursing and social care. Teaching and leisure are also highly female-dominated occupations. An important feature of these occupations is that many of them are in the public sector, so when we talk about women's work we need to remember that changes in public sector funding affect the numbers of jobs available. Similarly, around 65% of public sector workers are women, so any changes in public sector terms and conditions (such as the low levels of pay rises experienced by public sector workers since 2010) affect women more than men.

Women's pay is also an issue of concern in public debates. It is common for stories about the *gender pay gap* to hit the news headlines, especially as there has been relatively little evidence of significant movement to close the gap in recent years. The gender pay gap can be understood to be the relative difference in average gross hourly earnings between women and men within a company, a sector, or the economy as a whole. In other words, it is an aggregate figure; it looks at groups of women compared with groups of men. This is important. Just because there is an average pay gap between women and men in, say, a particular occupational group, it is not the same as saying that every individual man is paid more than every individual woman. New rules in 2018 require organisations to issue public reports about pay gaps between men and women, and this has ensured there is a flow of stories about high-profile organisations with large gender pay gaps. The Annual Survey of Hours and Earnings shows that the gender pay gap for full-time employees is around 8.6%. In other words, the population of women working full-time earn around 8.6% less than men working full-time.

Throughout this book we look at the choices that both employees and employers make in the labour market and how this affects issues such as pay. An important point to make in relation to the gender pay gap is that women often work in roles that are paid less: sometimes because of constrained opportunities; sometimes because of an active choice; and sometimes because of a complex mix of the two. So, the gender pay gap for *all workers* (in other words, combining both part-time and full-time workers) is higher at 17.9% because many part-time jobs are less well paid than full-time jobs, and more women take part-time jobs than men.

Around 15 million women work in the UK, and around 42% of them work part-time. When we compare that to men, we see that only around 13% of men work part-time. Again, the reasons for this are a complex mix of social expectations (especially about who provides the primary care for children and other family members) and occupational opportunities, including the fact that many female-dominated occupations such as nursing give far more chances for workers to have more flexible patterns of employment. That said, we also need to remember that the majority of women who work are employed full-time (58%). This is an aspect of the gendered debate about part-time work that is often forgotten.

How have these patterns changed over the longer term? If we look back to the 1800s it is difficult to get reliable data, but one source that gives us some estimates is census data. After 1841, occupations were recorded on census forms but there was very poor guidance for households about how to record women's work. Nonetheless, it became very clear that women across all classes were working in a wide range of roles. Common occupations for women in the mid-1800s included domestic service, pottery trades, cotton and wool manufacturing, metalwares, laundry, cleaning and retailing – a not dissimilar list to some of the occupations dominated by women today. Some of these trades were concentrated in particular areas or towns, so in those places the proportion of women working was very high.

Thus the notion that women's employment is a relatively modern phenomenon is quite wrong. Patterns of employment have ebbed and flowed as a result of changing social and economic phenomena. During the Second World War, women were actively recruited for a wide range of positions as men left for military duties. Women in households where money is tight have long been expected to contribute financially to household incomes. And one line of argument is that women's participation in the labour market is currently very high partly because of the currently very high cost of housing by historical standards. Looking to the future, it is probable that we will continue to see high levels of engagement of women in paid employment. This has quickly become established as a widespread social norm, even where women take the majority of the care and domestic responsibilities, and it would require a major shift of cultural expectations for that to change.

The service economy

One of the major changes in the kind of work that we do in the UK is from manufacturing and towards service work. Of course, manufacturing continues to be a very important part of the UK economy, the UK being the eighth largest manufacturing country in the world when measured by value of output. But there have been profound changes in the way manufacturing is organised which mean that, especially at the most advanced factories, lots of jobs have changed. Rather than relying on people to provide heavy labour, the jobs in manufacturing are now often about developing, running and maintaining sophisticated production lines with an emphasis on automated systems. As a result, the manufacturing workforce therefore only accounts for around 10% of UK jobs. Reflecting this, more of the 2.6 million workers in the UK manufacturing sector work in highly skilled roles, and a core focus of this sector is to develop a pipeline of skilled recruits.

The service sector relies much more heavily on people to deliver services and many of those roles are low-skill and low-paid work, such as catering, hospitality, care work and the like. The service sector now accounts for around 80% of gross domestic product (GDP), which is an internationally recognised measure of the monetary value of different areas of the economy. This is a big change from 1948 when the service sector accounted for around 45% of the UK's GDP. The Office for National Statistics recently looked at how the service sector had changed the UK economy over time and established that in 1841 the proportion of workers in the service sector was around a third (33%). In 2011 it was 80% and had grown pretty steadily over the period in between.

We work in a service-dominated economy. Most of the jobs we do involve some kind of provision of a service to people. This matters to the future of work because how we demand services as consumers will affect how we collectively change the future of work. We can see this very clearly in the retail sector. As consumers, we have demanded longer opening hours, often to fit around changing working patterns. In my lifetime, the tradition of shops closing on a Wednesday afternoon and on Sundays has gone from being quite normal to very rare and inconvenient to the extent that almost no shops would consider closing. But, of course, this has knock-on consequences for workers: shops have to staff more shifts; workers have to work more unsociable hours when other services such as public transport or childcare are not routinely available; and all the services to provide shops with their stock have to squeeze their operations into shorter closure periods, often leading to increased pressure on warehouse workers and delivery drivers. These changes are not good or bad; some workers will benefit, others will suffer. But they highlight how our preferences, choices and needs as consumers interact with the ways in which work is organised in particular sectors and industries.

The ageing workforce

Another common concern in public debate relates to the ageing workforce. It is certainly true that the UK population is ageing fast and this is changing the public policy context. But it is far less clear that the population of working people is ageing in the same way. Until around 2000, the employment rate for workers over the age of 65 was quite steady at around 5% of that group. Since 2000, this figure has been ticking upwards and is currently around 10%. This is equivalent to just over 1 million workers in the UK labour force who are over the age of 65.

The reasons are pretty clear. People are living longer and tend to have more years of healthy life, especially in their 60s. The law has also changed so that employers are expected to open conversations about retirement as a negotiated process rather than at a fixed age. It is also probable that there are financial drivers. Part-time self-employment is a much more important category of work for this age group than for younger workers, so there may be some evidence that work can supplement other incomes from pensions, investments and other savings.

Although it is clear that a small proportion of older workers are able to and are choosing to continue to work beyond the age of 75, it is difficult to know whether this is likely to increase. The figure has not changed very much in the past five years or so, and many workers in this age group are still benefiting from opportunities to retire before the age of 65 with reasonably solid financial benefits associated with occupational and company pension schemes, increased housing wealth and good stock market yields during their adult lives. It will therefore be some considerable time – if ever – before it is usual to find a typical 70 year old who is in paid work.

Changing migration patterns

Like most countries, the UK has always had a fluid workforce that has featured both workers born in other countries who have migrated here and workers who migrate from here to other countries for work. Nonetheless, the decades of the twentieth and twenty-first centuries have seen a number of particular patterns relating to migration to the UK that have had important effects on the labour market. In the 1960s and 1970s, workers from many countries that had previously had colonial links with the UK were actively encouraged by the government to come to work here in order to fill demand for workers in public sector occupations. This brought new groups of workers into the labour market and new challenges for them, often in the form of racism and discrimination. This changing demographic in part fuelled the demand for equal treatment of workers no matter what their ethnic background, leading eventually to the Race Relations Acts and today's Equality Act.

The legacy of those migration patterns means that, from the 1960s, the challenges facing the growing black and minority ethnic (BAME) workforce have become clearer, despite laws that require equal treatment of workers regardless of race, religion or ethnic background. Workforce data persistently shows that BAME workers experience multiple disadvantages in the labour market, ranging from greater challenges to get recruited (Resolution Foundation, 2017), lower pay (Resolution Foundation, 2018) and more limited opportunities to progress (CIPD, 2017).

In recent years, migration from European Union member states has accounted for the largest proportion of migrant workers. The Labour Force Survey shows that, in 2016, around 3.4 million workers in the UK labour market were born overseas, accounting for around 11% of the working population. Of those, about two-thirds – or around 2.2 million – were born in other EU member states. Citizens of all EU member states have the right to live and work in other member states as a core principle of the freedom of movement of labour. This freedom is argued to be essential to counterbalance the right of capital to move between member states. Without the right for workers to be equally mobile, there is a real risk of downward pressure on labour standards and the risk that capital (employers) will play off member states against each other to reduce labour rights. The number of EU citizens finding work in the UK has increased since the expansion of the EU in 2008, and these workers have largely been absorbed into labour market growth with little ill-effect on unemployment levels. Indeed, many employers would argue that this supply of labour has been essential in filling gaps in key sectors such as agriculture, manufacturing and hospitality. Of course, the UK's decision to withdraw from the EU will clearly have profound effects on this source of labour, although the precise changes will undoubtedly be an outcome of many intersecting decisions and pressures for both the workers who are already in the UK and future workers wishing to come here.

Other forms of disadvantage in the labour market

Looking at the changes in who works and what they do when they are at work, we see complex patterns of stability and change that make it difficult to tell a single, simple story about employment patterns. But what we do know is that workers with particular characteristics are more likely to experience forms of inequality and disadvantage. Women, BAME, migrant, older and younger workers are all more likely to experience forms of direct and indirect discrimination, and other groups are also affected. Data consistently shows that workers with disabilities, workers from particular religious groups, workers who are not openly heterosexual, and transgender workers can all experience forms of inequality and disadvantage. These *protected characteristics* are given special status in UK law and any workers who can demonstrate that they have been disadvantaged because of these factors can potentially take a legal case against their employer.

In practice, however, it can be difficult to prove that a certain decision or behaviour was directly created because of those characteristics. That said, employers have generally taken their responsibilities in these areas quite seriously, and it is now common for workers and managers to receive training in order to help them identify the potential for conscious and unconscious biases about particular groups of staff.

Labour share of income

One of the major concerns of observers and policy makers about work in recent decades has been a marked decline in the share of income that goes to labour (workers) rather than capital (employers). *Labour's share of income* is quite a complex economic idea, but at its simplest it shows us the relative balance of reward of economic activity to workers on the one hand, and to employers and investors on the other hand. Since the 1980s, labour's share of national income has declined in many industrially advanced economies (Dao et al., 2017). Although the fall in the UK has been slower than some countries – notably the USA – it has fallen to some-where around 55% of national income (for an analysis see Haldane, 2015). This is also associated with greater inequality in those economies because those at the very top are gaining more return for their investments than workers who rely only on selling their labour. It also has the potential to cause problems with demand because, if workers are not earning enough to buy goods and services, then demand drops.

The causes of the decline in the labour share of income are hotly debated, though it is widely agreed that the particular ways in which technology has been used are important. Technological developments in production and provision of services means that a lot of mid-level skills can be replaced, such as in factory work. Jobs that are classified as low-skill often rely heavily on personal interactions, such as in care work, retail and hospitality. These are difficult and expensive (although not impossible) to automate. High-skill work also requires more complex task interactions and although it is by no means impossible that some of these tasks will be automated in future, those trends are not widespread at present.

The fact that automation has so far mainly affected mid-skill tasks is partly what accounts for what researchers sometimes call the *hourglass labour market* (for an excellent discussion of the effects on workers see Holmes and Tholen, 2013). When we look at changes in the UK labour market, we see that high-skill work and low-skill work have both grown strongly in the past decade or so. What has seen much less growth are mid-level skills. As a result, the inequalities between people at the top of the labour market and those at the bottom have been sharpened. And the more people there are in the lowest paid jobs, the less of a share of income labour as a whole is likely to see.

Households

Until now, we have been discussing individuals, and this is often the level at which data is collected. However, most people live with and share resources with other people in family and/or household units. Most working adults organise their resources as households that comprise one or more income earners. Of course, the nature of these households is complex and always has been, but what matters when we think about work is that not everyone – and not even every adult – in a household needs to be engaged in paid employment to make the household resources sustainable. Indeed, it can be helpful to a household if there are people who can take on unpaid domestic responsibilities, or what is sometimes called *reproductive labour*. When we talk about work, we need always to recognise and acknowledge this very important unpaid domestic labour and the ways in which it inter-acts with paid work. In particular, we need to recognise that, even in a single-person household, paid work can only take place with the support of a great deal of unpaid domestic labour.

Trade unions

Before we move on to look at the future of work, we need to think about how workers get their voices heard. Workers can act as individuals, for example when they negotiate a flexible work pattern to suit their household and domestic needs, or when they agree to take on a new job, and they can also act collectively, usually through a structure and organisation called a trade union. The job of unions is to represent the collective interests of their members, and sometime of workers more generally. Unions are important in how and why work looks as it does in the UK and most other countries and although they have lost membership and influence in recent decades, they continue to influence the future of work, so it is important that we are clear about how they came about and what they do.

In response to the dangerous and exploitative conditions many workers found themselves in during the processes of industrialisation and urbanisation, one response was to organise together into trade unions. By working together, unions could try to redress the imbalance of power in the employment relationship, where the most important tactic available to any union is to take strike action. A strike involves workers collectively withdrawing their labour in order to pursue a particular demand or set of demands. A strike disrupts the activities of the employer and shows that even if an employer does not need an individual worker, it certainly does need the collective group of workers. This right for a worker to withdraw labour is now deeply embedded in international social norms and established as a human right.

The strength of trade unions and their ability to argue for improvements to work and employment have ebbed and flowed since the late 1800s when they became a popular and widespread movement for social change. Each year, the UK government issues official statistics on trade union membership and influence. The data shows that in 2017 around 6.2 million workers were members of trade unions. This number has declined consistently since a peak in 1979 when there were 13 million members. Numbers of members are not always a good measure of the influence of trade unions because the number of workers in the labour market changes. The proportion of workers is therefore often taken as a more important figure. On that measure, around 23% of workers are members of unions. This number has been collected only from 1995 when it was 32%.

Importantly, union membership is higher in the public sector (around 52% of workers compared with 13% in the private sector), partly because that is where unions are still regularly consulted and involved in negotiated changes to the future of work, and partly because this is where they are therefore able to demonstrate their effectiveness because of those structures. We noted earlier that the public sector employs lots of women workers, and it is therefore logical that women workers are more likely to be members of a union than men. So although union influence in negotiating the future of work has declined considerably since the high point in the 1970s, unions are still a very important feature of work in the public sector and continue to campaign on issues relating to the future of work in general.

The decline of unions is related to many of the issues raised previously. The shift to private sector service work in small workplaces has made it difficult for unions to negotiate across fragmented workplaces. But probably the most important reason was that, in the 1980s, laws introduced by the Conservative governments of the time were explicitly intended to reduce the power and influence of unions and had notable success in achieving those objectives. As a result of union decline it is probably fair to say that employers have more influence than they have had for most of the period since industrialisation, and although unions still do a lot of work to promote and defend the interests of workers, they have less power than in the past.

The ability of unions to defend and promote workers' interests is important because, as well as running general campaigns, they also engage in a process of collectively bargaining the terms of the employment relationship. Where it is agreed by both the employer and the workers that a trade union should represent the workers in the process of collective bargaining, unions try to improve, defend and enforce the terms of the employment contract. Any workplace issues can be collectively bargained including pay, pensions, holidays, shift patterns, childcare provision, and training. It is probably unsurprising, therefore, that where workers have collective bargaining, their terms and conditions tend to be better than in similar work where they have to negotiate for themselves.

Unions are also important in creating, enforcing and extending employment rights. Through a system of workplace representatives, unions often pick up cases of bullying, harassment and arbitrary decision making by managers. Representatives can then work to make sure that rights are enforced and that bad practices are identified and changed. It may seem counter-intuitive, but through these processes, managers in unionised workplaces often find it easier to communicate with staff and can even benefit from better managed workplaces. This is important when we think about the future of work. As we have discussed, work is constantly subject to negotiation and compromise by all parties, and the process of formalising and collectivising those processes gives the opportunity to create a *buy-in* from workers about changes that are needed as the future of work emerges. This is an important point and one we shall return to.

Summary

Although there have been big changes in the ways in which work and the workforce have changed over time, we can also see remarkable patterns of continuity and consistency. As we have seen, the ebb and flow of different kinds of workers into the labour market has provided an impetus to change laws and working practices to try to ensure equal rights and equal treatment. These dynamics within society and the economy mean that there is never a single, predetermined and uncontested direction of travel when we look at the future of work. Rather, how work has changed and developed over time is dependent on the interests and actions of a wide range of participants: workers, employers, governments, organisations such as trade unions that represent workers collectively, and even groups beyond national boundaries such as people who move between countries for their work.

The fact that there are many different groups with different interests and different amounts of power to pursue those interests at any given time means that it is nearly impossible to predict the future of work with any level of certainty. Rather, we need to look out for those ebbs and flows of different interests and different power dynamics because they help to explain why commentators sometimes get it so wrong when they talk about the future of work. In the 1960s, for example, it was common to predict that by the 2020s we would all have abandoned paid work in favour of extended periods of leisure time! That prediction clearly has not come to pass, largely because of the way that paid employment is so deeply embedded in economic structures and social norms. Nonetheless, there are some things that are already happening that we know will certainly have an effect on the future of work, even if the exact way they play out is not yet clear. In the next chapter, we look at those trends and developments and some of the debates they have generated.

what do we know about the future of work?

Debates about the future of work

There are many public debates about the future of work, and the current tone of discussion is one of anxiety about whether paid employment will continue in the near future. Interest in the topic tends to go in phases and is often marked by concern about what changes in work and employment will mean for people, for the economy and for society more generally. We are in a phase where there is a lot of attention being paid to a number of developments: the rise of robotics and automation; the development of what has become known as 'platform capitalism'; and the idea of a 'post-work future'. Alongside these concerns, a number of policy responses have attracted a great deal of attention, in particular the idea of a Universal Basic Income (UBI) which would distribute a basic income to all citizens regardless of whether or not they then undertook any additional paid employment. We also know that in the past 30 years or so, workers have lost a lot of power in comparison with employers because of the decline of collective representation through unions. This has shifted the terrain of work and employment in significant ways, meaning that more workers are insecure and not finding good-quality jobs. Although it is important not to overstate the changes, this is probably the reason why there is a great deal of anxiety about how the future of work will affect us.

All of these are interesting ideas and demand further attention, but the main message of this section is that some of the claims that are made by people who look at the future of work are overly pessimistic about the levers we have as workers and as policy makers to help regulate work both now and in the future. The argument here is that there are choices facing politicians, policy makers, unions and even workers themselves about how to address some of the likely future developments at work and how to minimise the worst effects. But it is also important to recognise that in order to shape really positive outcomes for workers and to smooth transitions to new forms and patterns of work, there would have to be a significant change of direction from the general policy preferences that the UK has chosen in recent decades.

At many points in the recent past the UK has chosen to take a light-touch approach to regulating work and employment, but this is a policy choice. In other countries, especially in the EU, different choices have been made which emphasise the importance of workers and managers negoti-ating agreements about these issues. As a result, and in combination with mechanisms such as laws and strong worker representation, changes at work are often implemented on a more agreed basis with some of the worst effects to society mitigated because the interests of workers (who are, importantly, also consumers) have been taken into consideration. The argument here is that, when we look at the likely effects of changes such as automation, for example, robots are very unlikely to take over all our jobs, but many aspects of UK skills policies are not designed to allow mechanisms for workers to retrain and develop new skills. This may well mean that automation does have some pretty negative effects for at least some workers. Those effects might be exacerbated if, for example, work-ers have very little influence over how new technologies are introduced. But we *could* design skills policies to help older workers to retrain and move into different occupations if their jobs change because of automation. We could require employers to negotiate how changes are introduced in order to soften the blow for workers. This chapter therefore looks at some of the pressures likely to face us all as we think about and experience changes in work and employment.

Work is a social activity

One of the central points of this book is to emphasise that work can only properly be understood when we see it as a social activity as well as an economic activity and legal contract. What does this mean in practice? It means that work does not just come to exist in a set form. Rather, decisions made by people shape the form and function of work: who works, what they do and how they do it. Some of these decisions are difficult to see and so can become very much taken for granted. When we apply for a job, for example, it can be challenging to imagine that someone in the company has designed that job: that is, what tasks need to be done, what skills are needed to do it, and whether the successful candidate will have those skills already, or whether the company will provide training. These are all conscious choices at some point, even if those choices were made a long time ago and therefore appear 'natural' or somehow 'inevitable'. Similarly, decisions about how much responsibility the state should take in developing employment skills is a policy choice and varies in different countries.

Understanding these choices and some of their effects on who works, where we work and how we work is at the heart of this book because work is often not a nice thing to do. That may sound a very obvious statement to anyone who has spent a day watching the clock tick down until they can go home, let alone for anyone suffering from one of a huge range of industrial diseases that can ruin bodies and minds, but it is so often forgotten in how we talk about work. More often, we hear companies tell us that *people are our greatest assets* and that the success of a business can only happen with the support of a wide team who are passionate about the company's mission. This can be true, but it can also hide a much darker side of work.

Emotional and aesthetic labour

If we start with the view that work is a social activity, then it is important to consider the social aspects of the exchange, and nowhere is this more evident than in jobs that require workers to engage with members of the public. As the UK labour market has changed, service work has come to dominate our experiences of employment. Front-line service work is different from production work, mining or agricultural work because it usually involves direct contact with the customer. This makes visible the process of consumption and puts particular demands on the service provider.

Front-line service workers often talk about the emotions that their work generates inside them, and how they sometimes struggle to control what might be seen by their managers as 'inappropriate' emotions. A restaurant worker who is confronted by a customer who is rude may feel anger, shame or embarrassment, but they often have to supress these feelings in order to smile at that customer and attempt to address the problem. This suppression of natural emotions can be exhausting and can lead to their spilling out in unpredictable ways, perhaps at home after a shift, or in a sense of ennui and cynicism that may even become depression.

This process of managing your emotions for the profit of an organisation that employs you has been labelled as *emotional labour* (Hochschild, 1983). Central to the concept is the fact that someone else profits from the process which makes it different from putting on a smile to meet your argumentative in-laws for a peaceful Christmas dinner. While there are similar processes going on, one is for profit and the other is to oil the wheels of social harmony. Emotional labour is a really challenging aspect of service work, and any quick look at the Internet will reveal a whole culture of memes that explore the emotional labour involved in service work.

As service work has grown, so have studies of emotional labour. Researchers have noticed that there are other social aspects of work that employers profit from and deliberately use to select staff. These can include *aesthetic labour* of 'looking good and sounding right' (Warhurst and Nickson, 2001) where an employer deliberately recruits staff who conform to a particular aesthetic that reinforces its brand. Of course, what this often hides is that potential candidates who look or sound different from these tightly defined expectations can be excluded from these kinds of work even if they have the necessary skills. Think, for example, of a retailer that hires young, slim, good-looking shop staff to wear the shop's clothes rather than older workers who may have years of experience in the sector.

Emotional and aesthetic labour are integral parts of service work and, because service work has come to dominate our collective experiences of work, are likely to remain extremely important features of the future of work. But they provide the basis of new forms of creating and reinforcing inequalities at work. 'Sounding right' can come to mean speaking in an acceptable middle-class manner, which can exclude many workers in a local labour market. Aesthetic labour can benefit people who present them-selves in particular ways and exclude workers who are different because of disability, ethnicity or even characteristics such as their weight. Some workers find emotional labour easier than others, and some people can find it difficult to supress their natural emotions if a customer is rude or aggressive. It is unlikely, however, that employers are going to become less likely to demand these forms of labour from front-line service workers. So, as we work in an economy that increasingly focuses on service work, these skills are likely to be increasingly in demand.

The rise of automation

It would be fair to say that workers have been concerned about the effects of changing technology on their jobs for as long as waged labour has existed. Probably the most famous example is the Luddites and their story illustrates a very important feature of the introduction of new technology that is often overlooked: namely, changing skills requirements. The Luddites were a radical group of English textile workers in the early 1800s around the time when new mechanised processes were introduced into textile manufacturing. The early stages of what we now call the Industrial Revolution had seen the development of various new forms of mechanisation and factory reorganisation that meant that textile manufacturing could increasingly be done by workers with fewer skills, and therefore at lower rates of pay, than by the artisan workers who had previously worked looms to manufacture cloth.

The crucial aspect of the Luddite movement was the context of hardship faced both by the skilled textile workers whose jobs were being threatened by the more efficient use of factory production *and* by lower skilled workers in those factories. The focus of action by Luddites was to sabotage the industrial machinery to show its limitations and weaknesses. In this regard, they were not acting out of fear as is often suggested in modern interpretations of their story, they were acting to try to increase their bargaining position with employers. Luddites therefore need to be understood as an organised, radical working-class movement protesting against the ways in which technology was being introduced and its consequences for all workers. Their protests spread rapidly and there were other examples in the UK and beyond of similar movements emerging in agriculture, tailoring and other occupations. Perhaps unsurprisingly, the response of the state was harsh, leading to legal trials and suppression.

By 1861, the government had introduced a specific law against industrial sabotage in a deliberate effort to penalise this form of collective action.

An important point here is that automation has long presented challenges for workers. Without organised structures such as a union or labour regulation to integrate and respond to those concerns and challenges, the implementation of new forms of technology at work can create tensions. In contemporary society, our concerns are about the rise of artificial intelligence (AI) and the increasing ability of robotics to take over even non-routine aspects of work tasks, though the future does not necessarily have to have a pessimistic outcome and there are considerable opportunities for workers to negotiate the introduction of new technology in ways that mitigate the worst effects on them. For those stories, we have to look to occupations and professions that are regulated and where workers have a strong voice.

More positive examples of the introduction of new technology are just as widespread as stories of resistance, deskilling of jobs and unemployment. They tend to be in workplaces where there is strong worker representation, usually in the form of a union. Unions are often able to negotiate that some of the worst effects of the introduction of new technology are offset by new working patterns, opportunities for workers to reskill and compensation to address some of the more problematic aspects such as changing shift patterns. In these cases, the technology is still introduced but the *way* that it is introduced is negotiated with the union representing the interests of the workers. Collective agreements about the introduction of new technology usually include clauses that look at how the work tasks of employees might change and how workers can be retrained to develop those new skills. There may also be agreements about how to reduce the size of the workforce if the new technology means that some roles will be replaced. This often focuses on ensuring that downsizing the workforce is done through not replacing staff when they retire or move on, rather through than large-scale redundancies. And if workers are made redundant and cannot be relocated to other work, there tends to be a concerted effort by employers and governments to make sure there are schemes to open up opportunities for retraining, and sometimes even to attract new employers to a particular area.

This kind of arrangement is commonplace in, for example, the German car manufacturing industry. We are all familiar with the high-end products of BMW, Mercedes and Audi. Many of these cars are produced in Germany using some of the most advanced manufacturing techniques. These work practices have been introduced through complex and ongoing negotiations between employers and the workers who are represented both by a trade union and by a works council. Those systems of representation are deeply embedded in the German manufacturing sector and provide a structure whereby the introduction of new technology can be negotiated to take account of different interests. This highlights an important point about new technology. It is not the technology itself that changes workers' jobs or makes them redundant. It is the choices that managers make about how new technology is introduced that leads to changes in the kinds of jobs available and who can do them because of the skills they have or do not have.

In the context of the current debates about automation, this matters a great deal, especially in the UK where organised systems of collective worker representation (mainly trade unions) have become very weak outside the public sector. Where companies and managers can introduce new technology with little collective representation from workers and their unions, there can be a tendency to look only or mainly at the advantages to the company. This risks introducing new technology primarily as a means of reducing costs and/or as a disruption to the market. It can be seen in the development of platforms that allow new business models to emerge which can challenge the way work is organised and how businesses make money in a particular sector.

Platform capitalism

The disruptive effect on existing business models can be seen in the introduction of some of the platform applications (apps) that have emerged in recent years, such as Uber, Deliveroo and the like. Of course, we can never know for sure what the motive was for developing these apps. It seems unlikely that they were developed simply to drive down labour costs, and undoubtedly they are providing a service that customers find valuable. But somewhere in the process of taking them to market and building a mass user base, the cost minimisation of labour has become important. This has been facilitated by the fact that in the USA (where many of these apps have been developed) there is comparatively little regulation of the labour market, light-touch labour law and very weak unions. As such, there is little pushback as these technologies are launched and there is little regulation of the labour that they use.

When new companies are launched to provide a product or service such as Uber or Deliveroo, there are not the same opportunities for established unionised workforces to negotiate the introduction in the ways they might in a German car manufacturing plant. As a result, there has been a process of organising workers in these new jobs and taking legal cases to establish their rights. Even in the UK, where labour regulations are weaker than in many European countries, it has been established that some of these workers are *workers* rather than *self-employed freelancers* and are therefore protected by regulations such as the National Minimum Wage, rest breaks and sick pay arrangements. This has forced a rethink of the Deliveroo business model in the UK. Of course, we cannot know how this will eventually shape up, but the example of Deliveroo shows how the introduction of new technologies can act to disrupt labour markets; even then there can be choices about when and where to push back against the tendency to try to deskill and deregulate work.

It is also important to remember that the introduction of new technology is not inevitable or following a simple trajectory. The UK car wash industry is a good example of where we have seen a mass disinvestment from technology towards labour. Some 20 years ago, most car washes were entirely automated with little or no human intervention in the process. Yet it is now difficult to find an automated car wash and hand car washes have expanded throughout the UK, often staffed by a small group of 5–10 migrant workers. Sadly, with strong pressures to reduce labour costs, car washes have also become places where there are pockets of informal labour and sometimes even modern slavery as it has become clear that there are opportunities for business to dodge many regulations, including labour regulation.

What the example of car washes shows us is that in a sector that is outside the gaze of regulators, labour can become so cheap that it can shape a disinvestment from technology. Tellingly, many hand car washes have set up in the spaces where automated car washes once existed, acting visually to reinforce the point that the robots do not always take jobs when the regulation of those jobs is very weak.

Universal Basic Income

The idea of a Universal Basic Income (UBI) has emerged and is gaining in popularity as a way of thinking about how to address some of the challenges facing us as we think about the future of work. The UBI has many different names: basic income guarantee, basic living stipend, citizen's wage, among others. At its core, it is the idea that citizens should receive a regular sum of money from the government which is unconditional. The income would either be enough to meet basic needs in that country, usually somewhere at or just above the poverty line, or be a partial contribution to that.

This is an interesting idea and has gained support in recent years, although it dates back to the late eighteenth century. Usually there are conditions placed on who should receive this income – typically it is for adults who can demonstrate citizenship. It is argued that the UBI can provide a number of advantages. One is that it can reduce, or even eradicate, poverty as all citizens are guaranteed a minimum income no matter whether they have a job. This is central to why ideas about UBI have re-emerged in recent years because it offers a way to imagine an economy even if automation reaches a level where some nation states can no longer provide enough jobs to provide a high level of employment for their citizens.

Much of this emphasis on the UBI as a potential mechanism to address the risk of job losses from automation depends on whether or not the spread of automation does actually lead to a significant reduction in jobs. I have argued that there is no simple link between these two trends. Even if auto-mation spreads to the extent and at the rate predicted by the most bullish researchers, governments and policy makers face choices about how they address those changes. There are plenty of examples where changes in automation in the past have been integrated into the work processes of existing employees. In those cases, the tasks within particular jobs may change, and it may even be that we see changes in the kinds of jobs available in a particular sector or industry, but wave after wave of automation has not resulted in a mass destruction of jobs within capitalist economies to this point. That is not to say that automation benefits everyone, and certainly not to say that automation affects all workers equally, but the examples given previously do show how changes can be negotiated and managed when the interests of different groups are taken into consideration.

What is perhaps more interesting is that debates about the UBI are being taken by some commentators to rethink what work might look like if capitalism itself was challenged. Some of these commentators are more optimistic than others. Erik Olin Wright (2009) was a leading thinker about labour issues and he argues that a UBI might provide a basis for workers to gain more power with regard to capital because it would decouple at least part of the need for workers to sell their labour power in order to live. This could give citizens greater opportunities to engage in a far broader set of activities, only some of which may be paid labour.

Other commentators are more pessimistic. They are concerned that a basic income might lead people to become lazy and not want to sell their labour power, or even to spend their income on things that are problematic, such as drugs. There have been various experiments over the years in particular regions and towns that have introduced forms of the UBI, but the data is very mixed. Overall, it certainly is not clear that these negative effects are widespread in the short term. Which is not quite the same as saying that if such experiments lasted for a long time, there would not be some profound changes in society and the labour market. However, the evidence does not generally show that there would be a sudden shift in behaviours.

Perhaps the most important lesson when we review evidence on 'big ideas' about the future of work is that we are individually and collectively deeply socialised into paid employment. Our societies are structured towards educating children in patterns that are similar to the standard working week and we arrange other services such as childcare and transport to suit those patterns. We also make social judgements about income and wealth: how we acquire that income, how we spend it, how much we save, and similar. When big changes happen, we often see narratives that emphasise the responsibilities of individuals. Think perhaps of the growing narrative that younger workers should make financial sacrifices to buy property which fail to take account of the massive structural changes within the UK property market that have seen prices inflated to tens of times the annual income of these workers. These narratives reflect deeply embedded perspectives of work, wealth and income which have developed across time, and particularly since the emergence of forms of advanced capitalism.

Those ideas have proven to be remarkably difficult to change in our societies and our views about how economies and societies should work.

So while it is clear that some changes will happen in the world of work, and that those changes will have important effects on the work we do and the societies we live in, they are unlikely to happen in easily predictable ways because many of these ideas about work are so embedded in the thinking of workers, of employers and of policy makers. This makes the structures of work and employment very *sticky* and often surprisingly slow to change.

Flexible work

Flexible work is another 'big idea' about the future of work that is often misunderstood. Debates rage about the pros and cons of flexibility for both workers and organisations and much of the evidence around that depends on what we mean when we talk about flexibility. A recent report has outlined many of the debates in considerable detail (Taylor, 2017). The review identifies seven main kinds of flexible working: part-time work, self-employment, agency work, temporary work, zero-hours contracts, multi-job working, and gig economy work. There is no equally reliable data on how many people work in each of these groups, and some overlap, but Table 3.1 contains some estimates which are taken from the Taylor Review.

Table 3.1

Part-time work	Around 26% of total employment. Higher than most comparator EU countries
Self-employment	Around 15% of total employment. Much higher than many countries but around the EU28 average
Agency work	Estimates vary between around 800,000 and 1.2 million workers
Temporary work	Around 6% of total employment. Approximately 1.6 million – including temporary agency workers
Zero-hours contracts	Data only started to be captured recently and has some issues with reliability and definition. Best estimate around 2.8% of total employment: 905,000 workers

(Continued)

Table 3.1 (Continued)

Multi-job working	Around 3.5% of total employment; 1.1 million workers have at least two jobs. May miss informal online platform working, e.g. eBay selling, renting rooms through Airbnb, etc.
Gig economy work	Very difficult to identify reliable data as problems with definitions. CIPD recently estimated 4% of total employment: 1.3 million workers

Source: Taylor Review of Modern Working Practices (2017)

Flexible work can be extremely beneficial to both parties. A common example in the UK is the decision by many people with care responsibilities – often, but not always, women who take the primary role in childcare – to work part-time. This flexibility can bring real benefits to workers who need more time to allocate to tasks outside paid employment by helping to keep them in the labour market. It can also benefit employers who can retain workers with particular skills and experience. But we also know that there are real downsides to the way part-time work is often implemented by companies. Too often the social norms of full-time work dominate the thinking and practices of organisations, managers and other workers and make it very difficult for part-time workers to limit their hours in practice. Part-time workers often speak about having to be very strict in reminding people that they do not work on particular days or at particular times of day, and many report feeling guilty about not being seen as an *ideal worker*. We also know that many part-time workers miss out on training and development opportunities. In principle, it is now unlawful to treat part-time workers differently when it comes to training, but in practice there can be a myriad reasons why some groups of workers benefit from some opportunities and others do not.

Similar arguments are often put forward about fixed-term and temporary work. Fixed-term work can be very useful for workers to build skills and experience working for different organisations. Equally, employers often need additional staff to cover a busy period, or to cover a member of staff on leave. What is more problematic is that in some sectors, occupations and industries, this kind of work has become much more widespread and can be used as a way for employers to hire workers on much more disadvantageous terms and conditions than core staff. Fixed-term staff often have few rights when it comes to dismissal and redundancies, so employers can use them as a way of hedging risks; if the organisation hits a difficult period, it can reduce the number of staff by ending the contracts of the fixed-term workers rather than workers on open-ended contracts.

This leads some scholars to talk about the *core* and *periphery* workforce (Atkinson, 1984). The core workforce can be thought of as those people who are central to the primary objectives of the organisation and whose jobs are focused on delivering them. These workers tend to have comparatively good terms and conditions, such as open-ended contracts, beneficial wages and other forms of remuneration, and some protection against redundancy. Peripheral workers are those people who deliver functions that are not central to the core business, as well as people needed to flex the workforce at times of peak demand. These workers tend to be employed on less good terms and conditions, often with lower wages, fewer benefits and less job security.

Although this can be a helpful way to think about things, it is rather simplistic because there are lots of different kinds of *core workers* and certainly lots of different ways people can find themselves in the *peripheral workforce*. A better way to think about these issues is to ask the question: why is an employer making these jobs flexible? If a flexible job has no disadvantage to the worker over a comparable role that is full-time and open-ended, then it is usually unproblematic. Indeed, it may well bring considerable benefits to the worker. But if a job has some kind of disadvantage then it is quite probably being used to the employer's benefit and may well bring problems for the workers who take on such roles, even if these problems are understood and accepted by the workers when they agree to take on the role.

No one would claim that all flexible work is bad for workers. That said, we need to acknowledge that a consequence of the complex decisions being made by managers and organisations across the labour market is that some kinds of workers are consistently more likely to find themselves in various forms of flexible work that bring disadvantages. In the UK, the groups who are more likely to find themselves in various forms of flexible or *precarious work* are: women (and in particular mothers), young workers, migrant workers and workers from BAME groups. The reasons are complex and not all groups are affected in the same ways. If we look, for example, at young workers, there are two main dynamics happening: first, they tend to work in sectors that demand flexible working, such as hospitality and retail; and, second, they often lack the skills and experience to be hired into the most secure jobs. Which, of course, begs the question as to which came first: did the hospitality and retail sectors design flexible jobs to attract young people, or were they able to make those jobs flexible because they hire lots of young people who are often not in a position to protest too much? The answer is an interaction of both. For other groups, there is more evidence that there are forms of discrimination at play. Young workers certainly do face discrimination in the workplace, but it is often argued that employers and policy makers need to recognise that young workers often do have less experience and fewer skills than other groups. For groups such as migrant workers, there can be much more explicit forms of discrimination and exclusion taking place.

Flexible work has grown in the UK labour force, and the emergence of gig work, self-employment and zero-hours contracts means that new forms of flexible work have appeared in recent years, especially in the immediate aftermath of the Global Financial Crisis when some workers were finding it difficult to secure good-quality jobs. The challenge for the future of work is to try to ensure that these jobs provide flexibility to workers who really need and want it, rather than only securing forms of flexibility that benefit employers. There are choices and negotiations that could help ensure that flexible work is good work that supports people as they navigate the labour market at key points of their lives.

The dark side of work

At its most extreme, going to work can kill us. For example, 137 people died in the UK in 2017 as a result of industrial accidents (HSE, 2018). The figures for injury and illness are far higher, with over 600,000 workers reporting non-fatal injuries in 2016–17. Relatedly, nearly 650,000 workers report experiencing acts of violence directed towards them at work, although the majority of those (over 60%) resulted in no injury. Industrial illnesses and diseases are also a direct effect of working in some types of environment. Examples can be physical, such as the risk of lung diseases for workers who work with particular chemicals or in jobs such as mining, and they also include mental ill-health such as stress. The Health and Safety Executive estimates that in 2016–17 around 1.4 million workers suffered this kind of work-related illness or disease. The figure is even higher when we account for the fact that some diseases do not show up until later in life and can affect people after they have retired.

These headlines tell us that work can be very, very bad for us. When we look more widely, we see that the dark side of work is not just about death, illness or injury. For many people, the daily grind of selling their labour is stressful or simply boring. Figures are inevitably difficult and contested, but it is quite well established that more than half of the work-force has at some point experienced mental health problems as a direct effect of their work, or where work has been a major contributory factor. Crucially important, over 90% of managers recognise that what they do affects the mental well-being of the staff they manage, so the choices about how work is organised are clearly recognised as important by the people with most influence in the process. Yet work is often a place where performance is closely monitored and controlled, which we know is a direct contributor to stress and mental ill-health. The dark side of performance management is well researched, and one academic goes as far as to call it the *new workplace tyranny* (Taylor, 2013). Workplace studies clearly show how increased pressure on line managers to deliver particular targets can lead to a reorganisation of work and rules that change working patterns and expectations.

And here is an important tension: people who make policies about work tend to have some of the best jobs, so can fall into the trap of not recognising how bad work is for a lot of people. Policy makers, politicians and senior managers all tend to benefit from well-paid jobs with more freedom and flexibility than most workers – despite notable performance pressures – so their experiences of work can lead them to have a very different understanding of what work is like. This helps explain why there is often a gap between the *rhetoric and realties* (Legge, 1995) of managing people at work.

Dirty, dangerous and demeaning work

Work can be difficult for all workers, but some have jobs that involve dirty, dangerous and demeaning tasks. Working in an animal slaughterhouse or in the sewage system might fall into this category. Importantly, so do lots of jobs that involve cleaning up after and caring for human beings, especially when they are incapable of doing those jobs for themselves because they are very old or very young. These jobs are often low status and many countries rely on migrant workers to do these roles because local workers are unwilling to take them. In these roles, there are tensions between organisations recognising that they may be able to hire workers for low wages, especially if those workers may struggle to find alternative employment, and needing to pay a sufficiently high wage to attract workers to take on some of these unpleasant tasks. Unsurprisingly, trade unions often try to recruit these workers in order to try to minimise the risks, but there can be real challenges if there are few other opportunities for these workers to find employment and they may not want to rock the boat by asking for better terms and conditions.

Importantly, in public debate these jobs are often discussed as being *low skill* rather than *low paid.* This is simply inaccurate as many of these jobs require very high levels of skill, and in care work, for example, high levels of emotional labour. It is important, therefore, that we think carefully about the idea of skills and why it matters to the future of work.

What are skills and why do they matter to the future of work?

When we talk about skills in the context of work and employment, we mean the knowledge, abilities and attributes that allow someone to perform the tasks within their job role. This seems a very simple definition, but it hides a number of complex ideas and processes. First, the concept of skill does not assume that someone is simply born with those abilities and aptitudes. Even some skills that are often referred to as *soft skills*, such as being personable and being able to resolve problems, are learned and socialised as a young person develops. Skills such as being able to use particular computer software or knowing how to fly an aeroplane have to be explicitly taught.

As a result, education and training are fundamentally related to the development of skills. In most countries there is a period of compulsory education that all children are expected to complete – in the UK, between the ages of 4 and 16. There are then mechanisms for young people to participate in additional education and training, some of which is provided by the state, some by educational institutions and some by employers. These structures of skills development have important links to the future of work as they are, at least in part, about giving people the skills they will need to enter employment. But we rarely know exactly what skills will be needed in the future, so there is always a debate and argument about how we can equip people both with the skills that are needed by employers now and how that may change in the future.

In UK national statistics, occupations are classified into four main skills levels (Table 3.2). This is an effort by statisticians to capture how long it takes for a person to become technically competent at their job. This is evaluated by how long it takes them to gain the formal qualifications to do their job (if any) and/or the amount of work-based training required. It also tries to capture the idea that people get better at some jobs if they do them for longer, so experience can be more or less important in most occupations.

Table 3.2

	Education and training requirements	Examples
Level 1 jobs	Compulsory education and/ or short periods of on-the-job training	Cleaning, catering assistants, hospital porters
Level 2 jobs	Good level of general education and/or longer periods of training and experience	Retail workers, machine operatives, drivers
Level 3 jobs	Some post-compulsory education and/or lengthy period of job-related training	Electrical trades, middle managers
Level 4 jobs	High levels of post-compulsory education and/ or training	Corporate managers, health professionals, teachers

Source: ONS Standard Occupational Classification (2010)

This classification is helpful because it allows us to link the skills someone has developed and the job they do. It makes clear that skills are an outcome of someone's participation in core education, any additional education or training they undertake, and the experience they develop as part of doing the role. This complex interaction between compulsory education, further/higher education, vocational training and experience is central to debates about the skills that will be needed in future.

It also raises important questions about who should pay for the development of skills and experience. Over time, there has emerged a general consensus in countries such as the UK that core education should be paid for by taxation and should therefore be compulsory. Although there are opportunities to opt out of state-funded provision, over 93% of children in the UK attend state-funded schools. Most schools, however they are funded, follow a curriculum that builds core skills in literacy, numeracy and additional subject areas. The exact subjects and levels of attainment young people are expected to achieve attract a great deal of attention and debate, but there is widespread agreement that compulsory education is intended to develop an intellectual interest in subjects as well as competency in areas such numeracy and literacy. The picture becomes more complex after the age of 16. In England, 72% of 16–18 year olds continued in full-time education in 2016, and if we include training programmes the figure goes up to 87%. This has increased notably since the 1990s when the figures were 56% for education and 77% for education and training combined. Of the remaining group, it is split about evenly between those who have a job and those who are not in education, employment or training (Department for Education, 2018).

This highlights a really important point that government policy in this area has widespread effects. That increase in education and training is explained in part by an extension of what policy makers call the *participation age*. Although young people are not required to be in school after the age of 16, there are statutory duties – especially in England – for schools and local authorities to track what happens to them, and there is an expectation that they are in education, training or employment. As a result, there has been a push to develop opportunities for young people and to follow up what happens to them.

Where the UK falls behind many competitor countries is in regard to the provision of post-compulsory education. In 2012 the UK was in nearly last place compared with other EU member states in regard to the proportion of 18 year olds in education: 63% of UK 18 year olds were still in education and only Malta and Cyprus had lower education participation rates. It is difficult to say whether this is caused by the generally low level of skills requirements for jobs in the UK, or whether the comparatively weak provision of skills has fuelled the development of a lot of low-skill work. And this takes us to another really important point about skills: who pays?

Most parts of the UK have moved towards a system that requires young people and their families to pay for large parts of their post-compulsory education. For most, this is largely financed by loans which are structured by the government and paid back over a very long time. Initially these were introduced for higher education but have been extended into many areas of further education as well. There is also a strong emphasis on employers paying for training, with levies on employers that are intended to incentivise them to develop apprenticeships. It is clear that, in England and Wales, there has been a strong policy preference for moving the cost of education and training away from the state and onto individuals and employers. Interestingly, this is an area where there is a distinctly different policy preference in other areas of the UK, and Scotland has taken a very different approach and retained funding large parts of this provision by the state. One intention of transferring these costs away from the state has been to try to get young people and employers to be more explicit and more vocal about what skills and education they need. It is difficult to argue that this has happened on a widespread basis, but it remains to be seen what will happen in future.

New skills: a collective challenge

One area where we face serious challenges as an economy and a society is in relation to skills. Employers worry about ensuring that the UK has enough skilled labour to create a labour market and economy that are strong enough to compete, and workers worry about ensuring that their skills do not go out of date so they can continue to work in whatever field they have chosen. When we add to that mix the changes that automation, robotics and various forms of artificial intelligence may bring to work in the coming years, we see that a focus on skills development is really important. Sadly, this is an area where the UK has long faced difficulty. For much of the past 30 years or so, respective governments have emphasised higher education as being central to developing skills, and vocational training such as apprenticeships have taken a back seat in terms of funding and quality regulation. Although that has started to change, there is still only patchy development of good-quality apprenticeships across the UK labour market. One effect of this is a real shortage of skilled workers in many areas of the labour market.

As a result, we have a highly polarised debate about the future of work. On the one hand, advocates praise the opportunities for robotics, artificial intelligence and similar to change the terrain of production and service delivery, with little concern for the workers currently doing those roles. Where workers are considered in these utopian visions of the future, it is often in the context of a *post-work future* imagining a life of leisure and meaningful activity beyond capitalism, often funded by a UBI. A more dystopian vision imagines mass unemployment, a lack of meaningful activity in daily life, and the poverty that accompanies it.

What is missing from many of these debates is a strong central analysis that emphasises the choices we have as societies about how we manage the introduction of these technologies, if, in fact, they prove as inevitable as many suggest. Choices can be made to prepare workers for these changes by reskilling them and investing in alternative job creation in sectors and places where jobs might be lost. These kinds of *active labour market policies* can be seen in countries around the world that compete with the UK and are typically managed by representatives of national and local state agencies working with unions and employers. Without strong voices of workers, it will be very difficult for companies, sectors and national economies to develop strategies that avoid some of most negative effects of these emerging technologies. Fears about large-scale unemployment dominate discussions because there are few opportunities for workers to express their individual and collective interests in the decisions about *how* jobs and tasks may be automated and what are the consequences.

The fact that the UK does not routinely create structures that facilitate employers and unions working together to consider the long-term skills needs of their sectors and regions is a policy choice. There are mechanisms such as Local Enterprise Partnerships (LEPs) which encourage a more strategic view of the economy and labour market in particular geographic areas but have little power in comparison with similar organisations in other countries. They produce useful data which helps guide decisions but have little influence when a major employment sector is under pressure, and it is not as common as in other countries for the parties to come together regularly to negotiate skills needs.

The skills challenge clearly shows how we risk losing out as an economy and as a society if we do not work together to plan and regulate skills development. It is in everyone's interests to have an appropriately skilled workforce that can meet the challenges of automation and other changes in the future of work. Yet the preference to leave these kinds of decisions largely in the hands of employers risks a *race to the bottom* where each individual employer cannot easily justify investment in skills in case workers are poached by other employers.

Who works: the challenges of demographic change

Demographic change will inevitably have an effect on our society more widely, and it will also impact the labour market very profoundly. Life expectancy in the UK has been on a steady upward trend for over a century, and despite recent predictions that it is likely to dip slightly in the near future, the effects of increased longevity will ripple through the labour market for decades into the future. The most noticeable shorter term effect is likely to be the higher proportion of older people in society, with an associated lengthening of working lives where possible.

It is important not to forget that for many older workers it is simply not possible to continue to work. Manual workers such as cleaners, or even nurses, take on many physical tasks that may not be possible for an older worker. Similarly, life expectancy is closely linked with affluence and class position. When we consider national policy making, this matters a lot. Pushing up the state retirement age means that many people will be considerably disadvantaged with comparatively short life expectancy beyond retirement age.

It is probable that an increasing number of older workers will continue to engage with the labour market beyond what we have come to see as 'normal' in recent decades. A report to Parliament (Houses of Parliament, 2011) predicted that a third of workers are likely to be over 50 years old by 2020. Already there have been a number of changes that are very likely to have the effect of extending working lives beyond the previously common retirement age of early 60s. The phasing out of default retirement ages from 2011, combined with an increase in the state retirement age, are already starting to have the effect of making retirement more flexible, although there is still work to do to ensure that employers facilitate flexible transitions. It is also clear that older workers face considerable discrimination in the workplace and there is likely to be increasing pressure to challenge this and ensure that, where possible and if they want it, older workers can continue to be economically active.

The ageing workforce also challenges ideas about how we might work in later life. The idea of a *job for life* has always been a myth for most workers, and there is little evidence that *job tenure* (i.e. how long you stay with an employer) has changed much in the past decade. Analysis of the Labour Force Survey by the Resolution Foundation (Gregg and Gardiner, 2015) shows that job tenure rose steadily from about 2001 when it was around an average of about 50 months in post to 2014 when it was around 65 months. The performance of the economy is a large driver of job tenure because people tend to stay put during hard times. But what is striking is that this data shows relatively long periods of service. Longer term data is difficult to analyse effectively, but there do not seem to have been major changes in job tenure over time and the cyclical performance of the economy is the biggest driver of relatively short-term changes. What is more relevant, especially when we think about older workers, is how they manage their transition to retirement. This is a function of many factors including whether it is physically and mentally possible to continue in the same role, the attitude of the employer and of managers, the financial resources available to the individual and, of course, simply personal preferences.

Older workers are increasingly common in the labour force and that is likely to continue as people experience extended periods of relatively good health into their 60s and sometimes 70s. What is less clear is how it might intersect with other demographic changes, especially with migration. The National Health Service is a key employer that is thinking very hard about how to plan for future workforce needs, and one particular challenge is the increasing difficulties with recruiting and retaining migrant workers. One response has been to look at the organisation of key roles and work out how to redesign tasks so that they can be undertaken by older workers. This again highlights that there are important choices to make about the future of work and that we need to understand them and to decide how to respond. Organisations and managers can choose to redesign jobs so that they can be done in different ways, perhaps assisted by appropriate technology. In the NHS, this has meant, for example, that some of the heavy work that involved nurses lifting and moving immobile patients that previously meant these workers had to be fit and strong (and therefore often younger) can now be done with the help of lifting devices and hoists. This helps workers continue in their jobs for much longer without risking back strain and other injuries. It also means that these roles can be taken by older workers. This is a simple example and it illustrates how we can change jobs and tasks to help workers as the society and economy we work in change.

Importantly, these changes to the tasks of nurses were introduced partly in response to workers asking for the changes through their representative unions and professional bodies. A combination of pressures such as compensation payments for back injuries, as well as the need to keep skilled workers in the workforce, has created a situation where managers and workers have thought more innovatively about the design of those jobs. This shows the negotiation and renegotiation of work going on and how here it is in the interests of everyone to rethink and redesign the tasks. More broadly, this example shows how new ways of thinking can benefit workers and employers, especially where those outcomes are debated and negotiated. In sectors and occupations where there are no forums for this kind of negotiation, there is a real risk that changes in the future of work benefit the stronger party – usually employers.

Pensions: the changing 'deal' at work

A further point raised by the ageing workforce is the issue of pensions. In the modern era of work and the welfare state, there has been a hope – and increasingly an expectation – that workers would be able to spend a period towards the end of their lives where money saved and invested during working years could be used to fund a period of economic inactivity. Retirement is, in fact, a relatively modern concept funded by a combination of the rising wages of the industrial era and the development of the welfare state which provided a collective funding mechanism for retirement income. In that period, employers were convinced to share the risk with workers and the state by developing company-specific pension schemes.

More recently, demographic changes have challenged the assumptions embedded in those arrangements. The notable upward trend of life expectancy is to be celebrated but raises questions about how individuals, companies and national schemes can manage investments effectively to provide an income for a retirement that is now often more than 20 years.

Add in the fact that many people now have periods of high social and health care needs towards the end of their lives, and the demands on pension income have become extremely challenging. Employers have withdrawn in large numbers from supporting investment schemes that provide an open-ended income in retirement. The state has responded to these pressures by increasing the age at which workers receive a state pension. Increasing responsibility is being put on individuals and households to manage complex financial products in the hope of providing an income in later years.

It is absolutely evident that there is a need for a renegotiation of the 'deal' between individuals, employers and the state about how to fund the period of people's lives after work. At present, there is an increasing emphasis on individuals and households to shoulder these responsibilities, leading to an increased risk of being exposed to shifts in financial markets and making poor choices. A fairer deal would almost certainly involve the state and employers sharing that risk more equally with the employee. Although there are many observers raising these concerns, there seems little concerted effort to make the kinds of decisions needed to head off potential problems.

Whatever the decisions of future governments, it is likely that these changes will have profound effects on the future of work. We are likely to see future generations who need to work longer before drawing down investment income, and it is probable that future working generations may well be supporting both older and younger family members.

Summary

This chapter has highlighted that there are some very serious concerns being expressed by workers and policy makers about some developments such as flexible work, self-employment and the way new technology might shape future demand for labour. There are good reasons for that concern and we must always be vigilant about defending and extending the rights that workers have fought for many years to gain. But I have also been careful to stress that these developments are not fixed on a certain trajectory; many of these trends come about as a direct result of choices by employers, by policy makers and by workers, and these groups have different interests. Sometimes those interests are in opposition to one another, sometimes they align. As a result, some decisions and trends are more contested than others, but it is always difficult to know how the future will pan out as different actors with different interests come together within a specific system of rules and regulations to influence the future of work and employment. In some respects, all we can say is that we do not know for sure what the future will look like. But we do know that some outcomes are likely to be better or worse for workers, and perhaps even for companies, organisations and for our economy and society more generally. We can say that some jobs are objectively 'better' or 'worse' than others and that key actors can intervene to make good outcomes more likely. The choices that lead to good work for more people are at the heart of what we *should do* about the future of work.

what should we do about the future of work?

Good jobs and bad jobs

Over time researchers have been able to identify particular features that make some jobs better or worse than other jobs. There is a lot of academic research in this area, and what those studies consistently show us is that, although there are some disagreements about exactly which aspects of jobs should be measured on any job quality index, there is broad agreement that *good jobs* share some common characteristics (CIPD, 2018). Most measures of job quality include objective characteristics of the work such as pay levels, other rewards and benefits; the level of autonomy and control a worker has; the terms of employment such as opportunities for training and progression; the extent to which the job presents both physical and psychological risks to health; whether workers have access to positive aspects of flexible work to help them balance their working lives with other areas of their lives; and the extent to which workers' voices are represented in decisions at work. They also include more subjective measures such as satisfaction with pay, the meaningfulness and fulfilment a job gives a worker, and perceptions of job security.

There are some important things to note. First, this is a pretty long list. Even some of the jobs that we might consider to be good may well not score highly on all of these measures. Think, perhaps, of a doctor. The medical profession is often regarded as including a lot of very good jobs, but many medical roles would be scored very low on the opportunity for positive work flexibility as many doctors work long hours with all the risk that brings to both their physical and mental health. Second, this list includes both objective measures (how much someone is paid, whether they have a chance to develop their skills through training, etc.) and subjective measures (how secure they feel their job is, how much fulfilment it gives them to do their job). It is now quite widely accepted that measures of job quality need to take account of both aspects because some jobs that might be classified as being quite poor quality at first glance can include aspects that bring real pleasure to the workers who do them. An example might be a refuse collector. Rubbish collection is undoubtedly a difficult and dirty job with some physical risks, early starts and comparatively low pay. But many refuse collectors speak very positively about the solidarity and meaningfulness they find in working as a team to make the neighbourhood a nicer place to be (Benedictus, 2009). So, both the objective features of work and the subjective features need to be combined in order to understand how people experience the good and bad aspects of work.

Measures of job quality matter to what we think should be done about the future of work. The example of refuse collectors is a really important example. It shows that although there are some dirty and difficult jobs that will always need to be done, there are ways of making those jobs substantively better. Throughout this book, I have emphasised that choices are made by employers and by policy makers about how to design work, and we can see with the example of refuse collectors that those choices play out in creating better or worse jobs. The choices of employers and policy makers are constrained and influenced by countervailing pressures such as changing demographics, changing cultural norms and, of course, the voice and power of workers.

It is generally agreed by policy makers at international levels that the main challenge with the future of work is to move towards *more and better jobs* (OECD, 2003) and this idea has been adopted as a central objective by organisations such as the EU and the International Labour Organization. That challenge has two related elements: moving existing jobs up the scale of job quality and ensuring that new jobs have more good features. Given the multiplicity of pressures faced by employers, including the clear need to maximise the efficiency and effectiveness of workers, external drivers and regulation of work and employment through labour market policies and pressure from workers' representative organisations are extremely important in moving towards that objective.

It is absolutely clear that the objective of more and better jobs must be a central policy objective as we think about the future of work. In the previous chapter, I argued that it is very unlikely that we will see a future where paid employment stops being a major part of our economy. Even if there were fundamental shifts in the structure of the economy and labour markets, we have discussed how work is a social activity which goes beyond the simple legal and economic exchange. Focusing on how we can improve job quality therefore not only is economically wise, but also places the human experience of work at the centre of our reflections.

Regulating the future of work

When we think about what should be done about the future of work and the quality of jobs available, much of the answer depends on broad approaches to regulating the labour market through law and employment policy. One approach is to say that the market should simply operate as a free market and if people want to sell their labour in very low-paid or dangerous jobs, then employers should be free to offer those jobs, and prospective candidates should be free to apply for them. In other words, money should be the regulatory mechanism where the parties can make judgements about how much to offer for a particular role to be undertaken and what level of remuneration is acceptable in order to do a particular job.

Relatively few people argue for a completely unregulated labour market because of the very real risk of pressure to do dangerous and exploitative work. But it is not uncommon to hear arguments that the state should refrain from extensive regulation because employers and employees should be free to contract without outside interference and that the terms of that contract can be settled in court if there are problems. This view tends to reject the points made earlier about the inherent imbalance of power in the employment relationship. It also assumes that all the necessary information is available to both parties at the time of agreeing the employment contract, which inevitably cannot be the case. In particular, it is rare for employees to have full information about the employment options open to them, payment rates are often not advertised at the point of applying for jobs, and job adverts do not usually list all the expectations of employees both now and in the future. When this lack of information is added to the fact that workers often find it difficult and expensive to relocate, or have commitments to a particular geographic area (perhaps because other members of their household have jobs locally, or because children are in school, for example), the imbalance of information between employers and employees means that it can, in practice, be very difficult for a labour market to operate as a genuinely free market. Thus, many of the assumptions that economists make about how markets self-regulate often do not hold to be true in the case of employment.

Starting from this perspective, countries around the world regulate work in order to avoid some of the most dangerously exploitative conditions that might emerge in a free market situation. Different approaches to regulation are crucial in how labour markets and economies will be able to respond to the pressures of future work trends. There are three main mechanisms to regulate work: laws, collective negotiation, and labour market institutions. Countries have different histories of how their specific forms of regulation have developed and emerged, leading some researchers to ask whether there are constellations of regulation that create better or worse outcomes. Of course, a great deal of the answer depends on what we measure, but we do know that there are institutional configurations that help reduce income inequalities, increase the share of wealth that workers accrue, and facilitate the development of high-quality skilled jobs. Generally speaking, countries such as the Nordic countries and Germany have systems of labour market regulation that facilitate pathways to high-quality jobs. These systems are typically characterised by strong labour laws, mechanisms that give workers and their unions a voice in how companies and sectors are run, and extensive systems of collective bargaining. It probably goes without saying that these systems are not perfect; they do not create equally good outcomes for all workers. In some of those countries there has been a significant growth in poor-quality, low-paid jobs in recent years, and there are often costs associated with these systems such as taxes on companies to provide training. But generally speaking, the outcomes for workers tend to be to create better quality jobs through strong mechanisms of labour market regulation and enforcement.

By contrast, the UK has chosen to take a light-touch approach to regulating work in comparison with most competitor countries. In practice, this means that employers have a great deal of flexibility about how to employ and deploy staff. This can have some important advantages and means that the UK labour market can generally respond very quickly when changes such as a financial crisis happen. One area of concern when we think about the future of work is that it means that there is little opportunity for employers to coordinate and plan their responses to some of the changes that we know will confront them, such as planning for new skills training and how to manage the transition of staff to new roles as particular industries and sectors grow and decline. Many European countries have systems where employers, workers (usually through their representative trade unions) and the state can work together to decide how to coordinate future plans. These ensure that there is some level of strategic thinking about, for example, the future skills needed in particular sectors and occupations. This kind of coordination means that the parties have to act cooperatively in at least some decisions. Broadly speaking, without some kind of coordination mechanisms, there is a risk that employers will compete against each other so fiercely that there can be pressure to make the terms and conditions of workers worse.

Why is light-touch employment regulation a problem for the future of work?

UK law gives priority to the contract of employment which is assumed to be entered into freely by both parties who are therefore assumed to be free to agree to the terms of the exchange. The real challenge with this approach is that an employment relationship lasts a significant period of time and is often open-ended. As a result, there are many areas of what happens at work that change and develop over time and which have to be renegotiated by the parties. Equally, not everything that happens at work can be anticipated at the point when the contract is signed. So, many areas of employment are not mentioned in the contract and are subject to the natural 'give and take' that happens in any long-term and open-ended relationship. When this inevitable vagueness about the exact details of the employment relationship is combined with the uneven balance of power that typically exists between an employer and worker, there is scope for considerable dissatisfaction all around and tribunals are often asked to make judgments about what is reasonable in a given situation.

Employment contracts do not have to be written down (although these days they usually are) and they are flexible enough to deal with the very wide range of situations in which people find themselves employed. Employment contracts usually state the basic terms of the exchange, such as how long the worker is expected to work, what they will be paid, what their holidays and rest breaks will be and suchlike. They also usually include reference to what happens if the worker or manager is dissatisfied, how any disputes will be resolved, and how much notice needs to be given if either side wants to end the relationship. In the UK, because of this preference for contract law, the state has had a general preference for staying at arm's length when it comes to regulating work. This contrasts with countries that have a much stronger assumption that the state produces codes that clearly outline what is and is not acceptable behaviour at work.

What is probably most important about the idea of relying so heavily on contract law is that there are systems to help regulate disputes called Employment Tribunals (ETs). The role of Employment Tribunals is discussed further below as they are crucial to enforcing fair contracts when the parties get into a dispute. Here the key point is that there is a clear recognition that each contract will be individual to the circumstances of the particular employer and worker. As a result, there is a strong incentive to try to reach a negotiated conclusion without asking for the judgment of an ET. It also means that the decisions of a particular ET are usually specific to that set of circumstances, so a ruling is rarely applicable more generally. As a result, there is often a default assumption that whatever workers and employers choose to do is fine unless or until it is challenged. This can be quite puzzling to many people if they find themselves having to navigate this process and makes it quite difficult to know how legal decisions may or may not influence the future of work.

By having such a light-touch regulatory environment, and choosing to remove many of the coordinating structures that encourage workers and managers to make joint decisions, the UK risks being ill-prepared for some of the changes ahead, particularly in the area of skills and job redesign. Earlier sections of this book highlighted how changes such as automation, flexible work and suchlike can be introduced through a process of negotiation between workers and employers. Negotiations about changes to work tend to focus on how to retrain and reskill workers so that they are able to continue to work in new roles after a change process. Where companies need to change the terms and conditions of work, these are typically rolled into the negotiations, as are any redundancies among groups of workers who will no longer be required as the changes are introduced. This form of collective bargaining can serve to protect workers from the worst effects of changes and can help companies remain competitive by having skilled staff able to take on new forms of work.

Because of the collapse of worker representation outside the public sector in the UK, there are few forums in which these kinds of discussions can take place here, which means that it is much more likely that changes will be introduced in the ways that benefit companies and without really thinking through the effects on workers. In arguing this, it is important to note that managers sometimes think about the interests of workers and actively decide to go in a different direction, but, more commonly, companies are focused on their needs and interests and the effects on workers can take a back seat. In that context of weak regulation of the labour market we can see why some of the looming changes to work seem so scary to many people.

What should we do?

There are four priority areas where the UK should look to strengthen regulation of work and employment in order to face the coming challenges more effectively and with a greater chance that the decisions made benefit workers as well as employers and managers. The next sections look in more detail at these. First, some employment rights only accrue to workers after a period of employment; at the moment, two years of continuous service. This is unfair and illogical when we think about the idea of basic worker rights. Extending all employment rights so that they kick in on the first day of work would help ensure greater fairness. Second, the input of workers into decisions both at work and in the national debate has declined dramatically as a result of the declining influence of trade unions. It is clear that this has had a considerable impact on broadening social and economic inequalities and means that the UK is often not well placed to address challenges such as changing skills requirements. Investing time and effort to rebuild collective voice at work is not simple but is very necessary if we want to increase the numbers of good jobs. Third, it is all very well having rights and agreements about how to shape the future of work, but if there are weak mechanisms for enforcing them, there is always a risk that they will not be implemented. The mechanisms for enforcing employment rights in the UK are very problematic and need to be strengthened. Finally, there should be an explicit extension of workers' rights to people who are not genuinely self-employed. At present, workers in this position have to argue court cases to establish their rights. This is a slow, bureaucratic and expensive process, and it is clear from recent cases that it is such a sufficiently widespread problem across some sections of the labour market that we need a new definition of *worker* to bring these people under the umbrella of standard labour rights that are enjoyed by their directly employed peers.

All employment rights from day 1

The state can exert influence in many ways and is sometimes talked about as being the actor that has power to set the rules of the game when it comes to work and employment. Statutory labour laws set the expectations about the boundaries of acceptable behaviour of both employers and workers. Statutory labour laws are passed by Parliament and outline the hard rules of the employment relationships – boundaries that should not be crossed. Examples include how much holiday workers should receive and minimum rates of pay.

Some of these laws, such as the National Minimum Wage and the right not to be discriminated against because you have what is called a *protected characteristic* such as your sex, age or religion, apply to all workers from the moment they start work. Others only kick in once someone has worked for a set amount of time. Probably the most important law in this area is the right not to be dismissed unfairly because of any other reason apart from your protected characteristics which only starts after two years of continuous service with the same employer. In practice, this means that an employer can dismiss a worker in the first two years for any reason *except* because of their protected characteristics (age, sex, sexual orientation, race, religion, disability, marriage/civil partnership, gender reassignment and pregnancy/maternity).

This gives employers a strong hand in the early stages of an employment relationship and means that some workers never build up enough service to be covered by these rights. Extending the right to have a clear and fair reason for dismissal to the start of the employment relationship would help build trust and security from the outset. This would not be to say that employers could never dismiss workers. Indeed, they could dismiss workers in exactly the ways that they now do with more longstanding colleagues: that is, through a fair process of identifying reasons why the role is no longer needed, or why the worker is not suitable for the position. It would put a responsibility on employers to show that the dismissal has been dealt with fairly, and this may require some additional administration, but that seems a perfectly reasonable requirement when someone is at risk of losing their income.

The examples given previously that highlighted how work is changing show us that as new forms of work and managing work emerge, there is often a public debate about existing regulations and the extent they should, or should not, apply to new forms of work. This is quite normal and can sometimes lead to new regulations or an extension of existing regulations. It is always difficult to predict in advance how these dynamics will play out in a given country or industry, but what we can say for sure is that where there is less regulation of work and employment in general, it is more difficult to argue that new sectors and new forms of work should be regulated. The other important factor in whether or not emerging forms of work can be effectively regulated is whether or not there are mechanisms for worker representation, usually through trade unions. Where unions are weak or absent, it will inevitably be more difficult to extend and enforce regulations to new forms of labour.

A stronger role for collective voice at work

As we saw previously, trade union representation of workers in the UK has declined dramatically in recent decades and is now mainly a feature of work that is either in the public sector (nursing, teaching, etc.) or in jobs that used to be in the public sector and have taken the strong tradition of trade unionism with them as they have moved into the private sector (railways, gas and electricity distribution, etc.). This still means that around a quarter to a third of UK workers are in workplaces where there is some kind of system for them to express their views and to negotiate with managers, but the majority are not. The effects of this decline are problematic because workers are now unlikely to get a say in how future challenges such as automation and the ageing population are translated into changes in their work, because there are few mechanisms to solicit their views. Even when they are asked, there is rarely an obligation on managers and policy makers to take account of those views.

In this context, collective voice becomes the only feasible way for most workers to try to address the power imbalance. While our employer can usually find a replacement for one or two of us, it would have far greater problems if workers acted collectively to express their views. The ultimate sanction is that workers can collectively decide to withdraw their labour by taking strike action. Although there are strict rules in the UK about how a lawful strike can take place, workers can and do take action collectively against their employer when they are unhappy with changes, or dissatisfied with particular terms and conditions of work.

Typically, workers bargain collectively – through their representative trade union – over terms and conditions of work, but, in principle, collective bargaining can be about anything that workers or managers feel strongly about. Different countries regulate collective bargaining in different ways, but in countries that have the strongest and widest forms like Germany and Sweden, it is common for the future of work to be a feature of negotiations. The exact mechanisms for agreeing how the bargaining takes place, what topics are negotiated and what happens if negotiations break down are highly specific, not just to the national regulatory context, but also to the particular culture and agreements at sectoral and organisational levels. Nonetheless, the point is clear: strong mechanisms for collective voice allow for a wide set of interests to be taken into consideration as decisions are made about how countries, sectors and organisations respond to the challenges of the future of work.

The UK has particularly weak mechanisms for collective voice and the result is that we risk making decisions about the future of work which prioritise the interests of organisations rather than taking into account the wider interests of workers and broader society. In order to strengthen mechanisms of collective worker voice, there would have to be many changes to the wider context and the regulation of work, but there is no clear agreement on how it could be achieved. It is clear that if there is not a strengthening of these mechanisms, we will continue along a path where employers' interests continue to dominate debate and decisions.

More effective mechanisms for enforcing rights at work

It is all very well having legal rights at work and even having stronger mechanisms of collective voice, but if there are weak mechanisms to enforce those rights and agreements, they have little real value. This is a real problem in the UK labour market. A recent study (Clark and Herman, 2017) showed that at least 2 million workers per year are not paid for work they have already done – either because they are not paid at all for that work, or because they are not paid in full for the work. Clearly, the right to be paid as agreed for work already done is one of the most basic employment rights both in the employment contract and in statutory legislation. The scale of the problem with this most basic of rights is shocking, and the study also shows the huge barriers that workers face if they want to try to enforce their right to be paid. Barriers include not knowing about rights, a lack of guidance and expertise in interpreting rights, and the time and cost of getting advice and taking a case against an employer.

More complex potential breaches of employment regulations are even harder to identify and to enforce. Not only do workers have to know that they have particular rights (and responsibilities), but also they have to be confident that an employer may be breaking the law. Trade unions can help to advise members, but they are uncommon in the private sector where employees mainly rely on overworked services such as Citizens Advice Bureaux to access guidance about the world of work.

If employees decide that they want to pursue a case to try to enforce a particular legal issue, they have first to seek to negotiate a settlement with the employer through a system of conciliation. There is a national service which provides advice and guidance to both employers and workers about this process, called the Advisory, Conciliation and Arbitration Service (ACAS). ACAS works with the two parties to try to reach an agreement. If that is not possible, the worker can take the case to an Employment Tribunal (ET).

ETs were designed to be a more informal version of a court and have legal status in a similar way to other courts of law. The role of the ET is to establish the facts of the case, to decide if there has been legal wrongdoing on the part of any of the parties and, if so, to decide on an appropriate way forward. A recent decision by the government to charge fees to access an ET has been overturned and while ETs can be an effective route to justice for some workers, the formality has gradually increased over the years, making it more difficult in practice to gain access to justice and redress.

Other rights such as the National Minimum Wage are enforced through mechanisms such as the tax inspectorate, namely Her Majesty's Revenue & Customs (HMRC). Health and safety issues are dealt with by the Health and Safety Executive; the Gangmasters and Labour Abuse Authority enforces issues of labour standards in agriculture and related industries; and other agencies are involved in enforcing and monitoring other aspects of employment regulation such as the Equalities Act. This adds up to a very complex picture where multiple agencies and bodies regulate and oversee different aspects of work and employment.

Regulatory complexity, especially with regard to enforcement and oversight processes, can lead to inconsistencies and a very real risk of under-resourcing. There is therefore a strong case for the UK to develop a form of Labour Inspectorate which could bring together all of these functions and demonstrate a serious commitment to regulate work with a coherent and 'joined-up' approach. Many other countries have these arrangements and they tend to provide a focal point for regulatory knowledge and expertise, which can prove invaluable as the world of work changes.

It is also clear that society as a whole benefits when workers are treated fairly for the work they do. On a basic level, an economy based on low wages and insecure work will likely be an economy where people spend relatively little and demand for goods and services slows down. But good work is more important than simply an economic exchange. Good work is a measure of dignity and respect for how we treat each other in society more generally. It is a signal that we understand that different people have different interests and that we need to discuss and negotiate ways forward that require give and take, compromise and discussion. If we accept that regulation of work is necessary as we look to the future, then we need to ensure there are mechanisms that deliver those objectives.

Extension of employment rights to bogus self-employed workers

One of the issues that leads to a great deal of legal complexity in the area of labour regulation is whether or not someone can be considered to be a *worker*, especially if they are self-employed in the kind of way described earlier: that is, contracting only to one organisation and perhaps even wearing the uniform of that organisation. When workers face this kind of complexity, they have to take legal cases to establish their status. While many of those legal cases have agreed that these people should be covered by legal regulation, such as the right to the National Minimum Wage and paid time off work, each case has to be argued on its own merits.

This is time consuming and expensive for workers, who are often not in a position to seek this legal clarification. Adding to the confusion, there are also different definitions of workers, employees and self-employed workers that are used in different areas of the law. One response would therefore be to overhaul and clarify the law in this regard and make it clearer which labour rights apply to which groups. This would be a major undertaking and would require a rethink of several important pieces of legislation that set the basic framework of legal rights for workers in the UK. But it would have the effect of making much clearer the rights that different groups of workers have and how they can seek a remedy if they believe their employer is not adhering to the rules.

Summary

When thinking about what we should do about the future of work, debate often focuses on the mechanisms that need to change in order to deliver particular outcomes. This chapter has taken a slightly different perspective and focused on the four main areas that would have to be strengthened in order to deliver a society and economy with more and better jobs. The mechanisms for delivering any of these could be quite diverse. So, for example, provision of Day 1 Rights could be delivered through changes to the law, or it could be achieved through stronger collective bargaining and mechanisms to enforce legally collective agreements. Similarly, stronger collective voice could be delivered through multiple paths, including strengthening legal support for trade unions, ensuring that bodies such as ACAS have a responsibility to promote collective voice, systems of minimum terms and conditions set through independent bodies, etc. Together these changes would help to build better employment practices, thereby ensuring there are more good jobs, and would also help to build a system in which workers' voices can be taken into consideration as future pressures emerge.

5

conclusion

A post-employment future?

Throughout this book, I have argued that it is very unlikely that we will see a time in the future when we do not have to work in paid employment of any form. Clearly, this is very unlikely within contemporary capitalism because producers of goods and services need consumers, and the vast majority of people rely on selling their labour to make those purchases. But this is not the same as saying that the patterns of who works, what they do and how much they work will always stay the same. For example, as house prices have increased, some people who have access to sufficient funds have chosen to stop working and invest in property instead. They accrue money to buy things from the rents they receive and the increase in wealth from the increasing value of the property as an asset. In a different situation, a household may also decide that not everyone needs to work in paid employment all of the time. So one adult may make enough income for the other to re-enter education or take responsibility for childcare, for example.

That said, capitalism is inherently linked to paid employment. Indeed, capitalism requires workers to add value to processes and products so that investors receive profits. So while capitalism exists, paid work will continue to exist. What this broad statement does not really capture is *where* that work takes place. Over recent decades we have seen a shift of a lot of low-skill manufacturing work away from the UK and towards countries such as China where the cost of labour has been lower. Those decisions are complex and factor in issues such as the cost of getting raw materials to the factories, the costs of moving finished products around the world, and judgements about whether the cost of labour in countries such as China may increase. None of these are once-and-for-all decisions and companies change their decisions as these variables change. In practice, this means that the jobs that people do in a particular country or sector will always be changing.

Nor does that statement unpick *how* we will work in future. As we have seen, there are many pressures that may change the tasks undertaken in particular jobs, how jobs are organised, and how we are contracted to do those jobs. In the previous chapter, I proposed some ideas about how we might set about developing a system which regulates work to balance the power between workers and employers more effectively. That, I argue, is needed because, without it, it is quite possible that the interests of employers will dominate the ways work changes. This has the potential to create very problematic outcomes for society more generally and there is therefore a clear need for a stronger say in how those changes happen.

Regulation of work

What we can do as a society is decide how we want to regulate work. What I have argued is that societies that choose to regulate work to try to integrate the interests of both workers and employers tend to be able to make decisions which mean that some of the worst effects of those changes for workers (and therefore for wider society) are mitigated. When workers have a sense that things are out of their control, that they have little voice in how changes affect them, and that there may be some very bad consequences of those changes, it is no great surprise that we see the kind of anxiety in the popular discourse about the risk of robots taking over all our jobs. What I have shown in this book is that we do have choices. The state has the option to regulate work directly, and/or to encourage workers and employers to debate, negotiate and try to reach compromises about how the future of work will play out. In short, then, while capitalism exists, we will not see a point where there is a post-work future, but we will see important – and probably sometimes heated – debates about how to shape the future of work. How those debates play out will depend in large part on whose voices are being presented and how much influence they have.

further reading

The Office for National Statistics (ONS) in the UK is a wonderful resource for anyone wanting basic facts about the labour market: who works, where they work, the hours they work, how much they are paid, etc. Much of this data comes from the Labour Force Survey, which is an internationally standardised survey of workers in the labour market, so it includes questions that can be compared across time and between countries. There is an employment and labour market section of the ONS website that guides users to lots of useful resources:

www.ons.gov.uk/employmentandlabourmarket

Where it is indicated that data is from the Labour Force Survey, the most recent version has been used, which, at the time of writing, contained the data for December 2018.

There is also a very good guide to the definitions and terms used when discussing the statistics of work and employment published by the ONS:

www.ons.gov.uk/employmentandlabourmarket/peopleinwork/employmentandemployeetypes/methodologies/aguidetolabourmarketstatistics#introduction

Data about the earnings of UK workers is available in a number of different formats and from several surveys. The ONS gives a good overview here:

www.ons.gov.uk/employmentandlabourmarket/peopleinwork/earningsandworkinghours

The European Foundation for the Improvement of Living and Working Conditions (Eurofound) also collects similar data for EU countries. It also covers particular 'hot topics' such as digitisation, automation, changing working conditions and similar. Again, you can explore its website and look for particular details broken down by countries, sectors and topics:

www.eurofound.europa.eu/

The International Labour Organization (ILO) is a branch of the United Nations looking at work and employment. The ILO has a fantastic international website that highlights important labour market issues and regularly publishes reports and other publications, many of which look at emerging challenges for workers, employers and countries:

www.ilo.org/global

Data about industrial accidents and injuries is collected by the UK Health and Safety Executive (HSE) which has a website full of statistics as well as information and advice for employers and workers:

www.hse.gov.uk

The UK also supports a body that is tasked with giving general employment advice for workers and employers called the Advisory, Conciliation and Arbitration Service, or ACAS for short. ACAS webpages are a 'go to' for many workers and managers who want advice about dealing with problems at work. ACAS also provides support for collective discussions when the process of collective bargaining becomes difficult. A look at its website will usually give insight into employment issues, and the helpline also gives advice to anyone looking for guidance as a manager or a worker:

www.acas.org.uk/

Data on trade unions can be found both in the official statistics of the UK government issued by the Department for Business, Energy and Industrial Strategy:

www.gov.uk/government/statistics/trade-union-statistics-2017

and through the Trades Union Congress:

www.tuc.org.uk

The TUC website is also a good resource about rights at work and union campaigns. It also provides links to its individual member unions that represent workers in particular sectors and occupations.

The UK has a body representing managers with expertise in human resources, namely the Chartered Institute for Personnel and Development, or CIPD for short. It is a subscription organisation, so much of its website is available only to members. But the CIPD regularly does research on work and employment and publishes press releases commenting on work and employment issues:

www.cipd.co.uk/

references

Atkinson, J. (1984) Manpower Strategies for Organisations. *Personnel Management*, August, 28–31.

Bell, D. and Blanchflower, D. (2011) Young People and the Great Recession. *Oxford Review of Economic Policy*, 27(2): 241–67.

Benedictus, L. (2009) The Refuse Collector: Trash Culture. *Guardian*, 24 October. Available at: www.theguardian.com/money/2009/oct/24/refuse-collector-trash-culture

Budd, J. (2011) *The Thought of Work*. Ithaca, NY: Cornell University Press.

CIPD (Chartered Institute for Personnel and Development) (2017) Addressing the Barriers to BAME Employee Career Progression to the Top. Report available at: www.cipd.co.uk/Images/addressing-the-barriers-to-BAME-employee-career-progression-to-the-top_tcm18-33336.pdf

CIPD (Chartered Institute for Personnel and Development) (2018) Research Report Part 2 – Indicators of Job Quality. Available at: www.cipd.co.uk/knowledge/work/job-quality-value-creation/measuring-job-quality-report

Clark, N. and Herman, E. (2017) Unpaid Britain: Wage Default in the British Labour Market. Project report published by Middlesex University, November. Available at: www.mdx.ac.uk/__data/assets/pdf_file/0017/440531/Final-Unpaid-Britain-Report.pdf?bustCache=35242825

Dao, M. C., Das, M., Koczan, Z. and Lian, W. (2017) Why Is Labor Receiving a Smaller Share of Global Income? Theory and Empirical Evidence, July. International Monetary Fund Working Paper. Available at: www.imf.org/en/Publications/WP/Issues/2017/07/24/Why-Is-Labor-Receiving-a-Smaller-Share-of-Global-Income-Theory-and-Empirical-Evidence-45102

Department for Education (DfE) (2018) Participation in Education, Training and Employment by 16-18 year olds in England. Available at: https://assets.publishing.service.gov.uk/government/uploads/system/uploads/attachment_data/file/718463/Main_text_participation_2018.pdf

Gregg, P. and Gardiner, L. (2015) A Steady Job? The UK's Record on Labour Market Security and Stability Since the Millennium. Resolution Foundation. Available at: www.resolutionfoundation.org/app/uploads/2015/07/A-steady-job.pdf

Haldane, A. (2015) Labour's Share. Speech to Trade Union Congress, 12 November. Full text and analysis available at: www.bis.org/review/r151203a.pdf

Hochschild, A. R. (1983) *The Managed Heart: Commercialization of Human Feeling*. Berkeley: University of California Press.

Holmes, C. and Tholen, G. (2013) Occupational Mobility and Career Paths in the 'Hourglass' Labour Market. SKOPE Research Paper 1. 13 January. Available at: http://www.skope.ox.ac.uk/wp-content/uploads/2013/01/WP113.pdf

Houses of Parliament (2011) PostNote Number 391. An Ageing Workforce, October. Parliamentary Office of Science and Technology. Available at: www.parliament.uk/pagefiles/504/postpn391_Ageing-Workforce.pdf

HSE (2018) *The Health and Safety Executive. Annual Report and Accounts 201/18*. London: Health and Safety Executive.

Legge, K. (1995) *Human Resource Management: Rhetoric and Realties*. Basingstoke: Palgrave Macmillan.

OECD (Organisation for Economic Co-operation and Development) (2003) Towards More and Better Jobs. OECD Employment Outlook. Available at: www.oecd-ilibrary.org/social-issues-migration-health/oecd-employment-outlook-2003/introduction-towards-more-and-better-jobs_empl_outlook-2003-2-en

Office for National Statistics (ONS) (2010) *SOC2010 Volume 1: Structure and Descriptions of Unit Groups*. Basingstoke: Palgrave Macmillan.

Office for National Statistics (ONS) (2016) Women Shoulder the Responsibility of 'Unpaid Work'. Article published on 10 November. Available at: www.ons.gov.uk/employmentandlabourmarket/peopleinwork/earningsandworkinghours/articles/womenshouldertheresponsibilityofunpaidwork/2016-11-10

Resolution Foundation (2017) Black and ethnic minority workers need a bigger living standards reward for their astounding progress in getting degrees. Published on 7 October. Available at: www.resolutionfoundation.org/media/blog/black-and-ethnic-minority-workers-needs-a-bigger-living-standards-reward-for-their-astounding-progress-in-getting-degrees/

Resolution Foundation (2018) Black and minority workers face a £3.2 billion pay penalty. Published on 27 December 2018. Available at: www.resolutionfoundation.org/media/press-releases/black-and-ethnic-minority-workers-face-a-3-2bn-annual-pay-penalty/

Roantree, B. and Vira, K. (2018) The Rise and Rise of Women's Employment in the UK. Institute for Fiscal Studies, Briefing Note, 27 April. Available at: www.ifs.org.uk/publications/12951

Taylor, M. (2017) Good Work: The Taylor Review of Modern Working Practices. Available at: https://assets.publishing.service.gov.uk/government/uploads/system/uploads/attachment_data/file/627671/good-work-taylor-review-modern-working-practices-rg.pdf

Taylor, P. (2013) Performance Management and the New Workplace Tyranny: A Report for the Scottish Trades Union Congress. Publicly available report at: https://strathprints.strath.ac.uk/57598/

Warhurst, C. and Nickson, D. (2001) *Looking Good, Sounding Right*. London: Industrial Society.

Wright, E. O. (2009) *Envisioning Real Utopias*. London: Verso.

index